# The Montgomery County

## ❦ Maryland ❦

From Its
### Earliest Settlement in 1650 to 1879:

THE EARLIEST LAND GRANTS.—BY WHOM PATENTED.—THEIR ORDER OF
SETTLEMENT AND PRESENT OWNERS.—LOCAL AND GENERAL
EVENTS.—LEADING INCIDENTS.—PRINCIPAL TOWNS,
VILLAGES, &C.—ITS SOIL, PRODUCTS, AND
INDUSTRIES. ALSO,

SKETCHES OF THE PROMINENT MEN OF THE COUNTY.

# DIRECTORY

OF POST OFFICES, MERCHANTS, MANUFACTURERS, PROFESSORS,
FARMERS, TOBACCO PLANTERS, MECHANICS, MILLS,
COLLEGES, SCHOOLS, AND CHURCHES.

## WITH AN APPENDIX,

CONTAINING A DESCRIPTION OF THE PROMINENT BUSINESS HOUSES
OF WASHINGTON AND GEORGETOWN.

COMPILED AND ARRANGED FROM AUTHENTIC SOURCES,
BY
# T. H. S. Boyd

*Clarksburg, Montgomery County, Maryland*

## HERITAGE BOOKS
## 2008

# HERITAGE BOOKS
## *AN IMPRINT OF HERITAGE BOOKS, INC.*

## Books, CDs, and more—Worldwide

For our listing of thousands of titles see our website
at
www.HeritageBooks.com

A Facsimile Reprint
Published 2008 by
HERITAGE BOOKS, INC.
Publishing Division
100 Railroad Ave. #104
Westminster, Maryland 21157

Originally Published
Clarksburg, 1879

International Standard Book Number: 978-0-7884-1995-9

# PREFACE.

In offering the present history to the public and the citizens of Montgomery County, it appears necessary for the publisher to present the motive that induced him to undertake the publication.

During the Centennial year of our National Independence, the President of the United States issued a Proclamation, requesting the people to assemble in their respective towns and counties, and rescue from obscurity and oblivion the incidents and events connected with the first century of the Nation.

Previous to the issue of this proclamation, the people of Montgomery County had resolved to celebrate the one hundredth anniversary of the organization of the County, on the Fair Grounds, at Rockville, September 6th, 1876. Speeches were delivered by A. B. Davis, Esq., T. Anderson, Esq., Judge Richard J. Bowie, Judge Pearre, Judge Jones, and others. The exhibition buildings of the Fair Grounds were filled with relics and curiosities, giving a faithful reflex of the past.

The object in the publication of this volume is to collect and arrange the materials, with such an arrangement of the matter as to give a true and faithful history of the County, in as concise and succinct style as the subject will admit; commencing with a brief sketch of the manners and customs of the aborigines, who once inhabited this region of country, and continuing with the earlier settlements by the whites, down through the period of the Revolution and the peaceful times that followed until the present, including geological features, streams, natural curiosities, general statistics, taxable property, synopsis of census, public improvements, towns, villages and post offices, with biographical sketches of distinguished persons, immigration and its effects, agriculture, pomology, and the culture of bees. Also, a complete Directory of Merchants, Farmers, Planters, Mechanics, Professions, etc., with a copious Appendix, containing sketches of the prominent mercantile and manufacturing interests of Baltimore and the District of Columbia, which are identified with the prosperity of Montgomery County.

The publisher takes pleasure in tendering his unfeigned acknowledgments to all those who have contributed material for this publication; especially to William Grady, Esq., the efficient County Surveyor.

T. H. S. BOYD.

# CONTENTS.

—◆—

## DIRECTORY OF TOWNS AND VILLAGES,

INCLUDING THE POST OFFICE ADDRESS OF MERCHANTS, FARMERS, &C.

---

# DIRECTORY OF PROMINENT MERCANTILE FIRMS.

## GEORGETOWN, D. C.

## WASHINGTON, D. C.

## FREDERICK, MD.

# HISTORY

OF

# MONTGOMERY COUNTY, MD.

## CHAPTER I.

### THE ABORIGINES OR INDIANS.

*Their customs and habits. Treatment of strangers. Treatment of enemies. Their vices. Marriages. Indian huts or wigwams. Dress. Religious ceremonies, etc.*

WHEN the Europeans first came to this country, they found the Western Continent inhabited by numerous nations, to whom was applied the name, though erroneously, Indians. This name was given to the aborigines of this continent under the mistaken notion of Columbus, in supposing that he had arrived at the eastern shore of India.

Touching the origin of the Indians, or by what means they came from the OLD WORLD to the NEW, has never been satisfactorily answered, notwithstanding that voluminous disquisitions have been written on the subject.

A majority who have investigated this subject agree, that Tartary, in Asia, is the native country of all American Indians. The region of country of which this history treats was inhabited by the Yoacomicos, Anacostians, Piscataways, Senecas and Patuxents, about the time of the first settlement in 1635. All of these tribes belonged or were under the control of the Six Nations, the central power of which was located in the State of New York. The Piscataways and the Nacostines or Anacostians, a tributary tribe of the Piscataways, resembled each

2

other as to their bodily and mental qualifications. In person, slender, middle-sized, handsome and straight. The women however, were short, not so handsome, and clumsy in appearance. The skin of a reddish brown or yellowish brown, hair straight and jet black.

In common life and conversation the Indians observed great decency. They usually treated one another and strangers with kindness and civility, and without empty compliments. In the converse of both sexes the greatest decency and propriety were observed. They were sociable and friendly, difference of rank with all its consequences was not to be found among the Indians. They were equally noble and free. The only difference consisted in wealth, age, dexterity, courage and office. They were hospitable to strangers. To refuse the act or kind offices of hospitality, was looked upon as a flagrant violation of a laudable practice in vogue among the tawny sons of the forest. Hospitality, they considered a most sacred duty, from which none were exempt. "Whoever," said they, "refuses relief to any one, commits a grievous offence, and not only makes himself detested and abhorred by all, but liable to revenge from the injured person." In their conduct towards their enemies they were "bloody cruel," and when exasperated, nothing but the blood of their enemy could assuage or allay anger, which rankled concealed in their bosom, waiting only for a convenient opportunity to strike the fearful blow, inflicted with fury that knew no bounds. So determined on revenge upon their enemies were they, that they would solemnly enjoin it upon their friends and posterity to resent the injuries done them. The longest space of time, the most remote place of refuge, afforded no security to an Indian's enemy.

Drunkenness, after the whites commenced to deal with them, was a common vice. It was not confined, as it is in a great measure at this day, among the whites, to the male sex, but the Indian female as well as the male, was infatuated alike with the love of strong drink, for neither of them knew bounds to their desires. They drank while they had whiskey, or could swallow it down. Drunkenness was a vice, and attended with many serious consequences, and often resulted in murder and death—this was not punishable among them, it was a fashionable vice. Stealing, lying, adultery and cheating, principally the offspring of drunkenness, were considered as heinous and scandalous offences, and were punished in various ways.

The Anacostians and Piscataways married early in life; the men usually at eighteen, and the women at fourteen, but never married near relations. If an Indian man wished to marry, he sent a present to the nearest relations of the person he had fixed upon, consisting of blankets, cloth, linen, and occasionally a few belts of Wampum. If he that made the present, and the present pleased, the matter was formally proposed to the girl, and if the other party chose to decline the proposal, they returned the present by way of a friendly negative. After the marriage, the present made by the suitor was divided among the friends of the young wife. These returned the civility by a present of Indian corn, beans, kettles, baskets, hatchets, etc., brought in solemn procession into the hut of the newly married couple. The latter commonly lodged in a friend's house till they could erect a dwelling of their own. An Indian hut was constructed in the following manner: they peeled the trees abounding in sap, then cutting the bark into pieces of six or eight feet in length, they laid heavy stones upon them, that they might become flat and even in drying. The frame of the hut was made by driving poles into the ground and strengthening them by cross-beams. This frame was covered both inside and outside, with the pieces of bark that had been prepared for that purpose, and fastened tight with the bast of withes of hickory. The roof ran upon a ridge and was covered the same way. An opening was left in the roof to let the smoke pass through, and one in the side as a door, which was fastened with neither lock nor bolt; a stick leaning against it on the outside as a token that no one was at home, was the only bolt to prevent intruders.

There was some difference in the huts of the Piscataways and Anacostians; the roofs of the former being angular, and that of the latter round or arched; the Piscataway families preferring to live separately, their huts were small; the Anacostians preferred to live together,—they built their houses long, with several fire-places, and corresponding openings in the roof and sides. In their dress they displayed more singularity than art. The men wore a blanket which hung loose over their shoulders, and generally went bareheaded. The dress which distinguished the women, was a petticoat fastened tight about the hips and hang-

ing down a little below the knees. A longer one would have
proved an incumbrance in walking through the woods or working
in the fields.

As soon as a child was born it was laid upon a board or
straight piece of bark, covered with moss, and wrapped up in
a skin or piece of cloth, and when the mother was engaged in
her house-work, this rude cradle or bed was hung to a peg or
branch of a tree. Their children they educated, to fit them to
get through the world as did their fathers. They instructed
them in a religion, in which they believed that *Manito*, their
God, "The Good Spirit," could be propitiated by sacrifices,
hence they observed a great many superstitious and idolatrous
ceremonies. At their general and solemn sacrifices the oldest
men performed the offices of priests; but in private parties, each
man brought a sacrifice and offered it himself as priest. Instead
of a temple, they fitted up a large dwelling house for the
purpose.

# CHAPTER II.

## THE INDIANS—CONTINUED.

*Their amusements. War Dances. Hunting and fishing their chief employment. Dances. The Calumet. Diseases. The medicine men or doctors. Death and burials. Lord's Prayer in their native language, etc.*

WHEN at home they had their amusements, their favorite one was dancing. The common dance was held either in a large house or in an open field around a fire. In dancing they formed a circle, and always had a leader, to whom the whole company attended. The men went before and the women closed the circle. The latter danced with great decency, and as if they had engaged in the most serious business. While thus engaged they never spoke a word to the men, much less joked with them, which would have injured their character.

They neither skipped nor jumped, but placed one foot lightly forward and then backward, yet so as to advance gradually till they reached a certain spot, and then retired in the same manner. They kept their bodies straight and their arms hanging down close to their sides. But the men shouted, leaped and stamped with such violence, that the ground trembled under their feet. Their extreme agility and lightness of foot was never shown to more advantage than in dancing. Their whole music consisted in a single drum, which was made of an old barrel or kettle, or the lower end of a hollow tree, covered with a thin deer skin, and beaten with one stick. Its sound was not however agreeable, and served only to mark the time, which the Indians when dancing, even in large numbers, kept with due exactness. When they had finished one round they took some rest, but during this time the drummer continued to sing until another dance commenced. These dances in keeping with that spirit lasted until midnight.

Another kind of dance was only attended by men. Each rose in his turn and danced with great agility and boldness, extolling their own or their father's great deeds in a song, to which all beat time by a monotonous, rough note, which was given out with great vehemence at the commencement of each bar. The war dance, which was always held either before or after a campaign was dreadful to behold. None took part in it but the warriors themselves. They appeared armed as if going to battle. One carried his gun or hatchet, another a long knife, the third, a tomahawk, the fourth, a large club, or they all appeared armed with tomahawks; these they brandished in the air to show how they intended to treat their enemies. They affected such an air of anger and fury on these occasions that it made a spectator shudder to behold them. A chief led them in the dance, and sang the warlike deeds of himself or his ancestors. At the end of every celebrated feat of valor, he wielded his tomahawk with all his strength against a post fixed in the ground. He was then followed by the rest, each finished his round by a blow against the post. They then danced altogether, and this was the most frightful scene. They affected the most horrible and dreadful gestures, threatened to beat, cut and stab each other. They were however amazingly dexterous in avoiding the threatened danger. To complete the horror of the scene they howled as dreadfully as if in actual fight, so that they appeared as raving madmen. During the dance they sometimes sounded a kind of fife made of reed, which had a shrill and disagreeable note. They sometimes used the war dance in times of peace, with a view to celebrate the deeds of their heroic chiefs in a solemn manner. The sacrificial dance was held at the solemnization of their sacrifices.

Hunting and fishing constituted their chief employment, depending on this as they did for a supply of food principally taken in the chase, and next to war, was considered the most honorable. They were experienced hunters, their boys were trained to this business, whom they taught when quite young, to climb trees, both to catch birds and to exercise their sight, which by this method was rendered so quick that in hunting they saw objects at an amazing distance. In detecting and pursuing game they almost exceeded the best trained dog in following its course. The principal weapons used by the Indian hunters were bows and arrows, some had rifles. Their hunting excursions sometimes continued for months. The Potomac River furnished an abundant supply of fish for those who were fond of piscatorial pursuits. Henry Fleet, who was the first navigator who ascended the Potomac River to the head of navigation, in 1625, describes the country as abounding in game, such as deer, buffaloes, bears and turkeys, while the river abounded in all kinds of fish,—the Indians commonly catching thirty sturgeon in one night. If in their travels they had occasion to pass a deep river, they set about immediately and built a canoe, by taking a long piece of bark of proportionate breadth, to which they gave the proper form by fastening it to ribs of light wood, bent so as to suit the occasion. The Indians, like all human flesh, were heirs of disease. The most common was pleurisy, weakness and pains in the stomach and breast, consumption, diarrhœa, rheumatism, ague, inflammatory fevers, and occasionally the small-pox made dreadful ravages among them. Their general remedy for all their disorders, small or great, was a sweat. For this purpose they had in every village an oven, situated at some distance from the dwellings, built of stakes and boards, covered with sods, or, were dug in the side of a hill, and heated with some red hot stones. Into this the patient crept naked and in a short time was thrown into a profuse perspiration. As soon as the patient felt too hot, he crept out and immediately plunged himself into a river or some cold water, where he continued about thirty seconds, and then went again into the oven. After having performed this operation three times successively, he smoked his pipe with composure, and in many cases a cure was completely effected. Indian doctors never applied medicines without accompanying them with mysterious ceremonies to make their effect appear supernatural. A missionary, who was present on an occasion when an Indian physician had been sent for to see a patient, says: "He had on a large bear skin, so that his arms were covered with the fore legs, his feet with the hind legs, and his head entirely concealed in the bear's head, with the addition of glass eyes. He came in this attire with a calabash in his hand, accompanied by a great crowd of people, into the patient's hut, singing and dancing, when he grasped a hand-

full of hot ashes, and scattering them into the air with a horrid
noise, approached the patient and began to play several leger-
demain tricks with small bits of wood, by which he pretended
to be able to restore him to health." The principal remedies
used by the Indians in curing diseases were, such as rattlesnake
root, the skins of rattlesnakes dried and pulverized, thorny ash,
toothache tree, tulip tree, dogwood, wild laurel, sassafras, elder,
poison ash, winter green, liverwort, Virginia poke, jalap, sarsa-
parilla, Scobians or devil's bit, blood wort, cuckoopint, and
others.  Immediately after the death of an Indian the corpse
was dressed in a new suit, with the face and shirt painted red,
and laid upon a mat or skin, in the middle of the hut.  The
arms and effects of the deceased are then piled up near the
body; in the evening, soon after sunset, and in the morning,
before daybreak, the female relations and friends assemble
around the corpse to mourn over it.  Their lamentations are
loud in proportion to the love and the esteem they bore the
deceased, or to his rank, or the pains he suffered in dying, and
they are daily repeated till his interment.  The burying places
are some distance from the dwellings.  The graves were generally dug by old women, as the young people abhorred this kind
of work.  Before they had hatchets and other tools, they used
to line the inside of the grave with the bark of trees; but afterwards they usually placed three boards, not nailed together,
over the grave in such a manner that the corpse lay between
them, a fourth board was placed as a cover, and then the grave
was filled with earth.  Now and then a proper coffin was procured.  The language of the two tribes had an agreeable sound
both in conversation and public delivery, although there was
great difference between the two.  The pronunciation, say those
who were skilled in the tongue, was quite easy.  The following
is the Lord's Prayer, in the language of the Piscataways.

"Sougwaucha caurounkyauga leh Sutaro an Saul woney
aoita, es a sawaneyou okettanhsela ebueawoung, na carounky-
auga nugh woushauga, neallewehue salauga tangwounant
oranoatoughsick tontaugwelee wheyon stoung chencyent cha-
quatant aleywhey oust anna thughsang long wass areuch tawan
tottenan galoughtounga, nysawne Sascheautang whss conteh-
sale paungaekaw, esa sawauneyou, esa sashautzta, esa soung
wasoung cheuneaw houngwa, anwen."

Their language was lofty, yet narrow, somewhat like the Hebrew, in signification full; like short-hand in writing, one word served in the place of three, and the rest were supplied by the understanding of the hearer. Their language was also highly figurative. The following specimens may offer an idea of their metaphors: "The sky is overcast with dark, blustering clouds," meaning we shall have troublesome times; we shall have war. "We shall lift up the hatchet,"—we shall have war. "The path is already shut up,"—war has began. "The rivers run with blood,"—war rages in the country. "To bury the the hatchet,"—to conclude peace. "You did not make me strong,"—you gave me nothing. "Look this way,"—join our party. "I will pass one night yet at this place,"—I will stay one year at this place.

# CHAPTER III.

*The Founder of Maryland. Granting of the Charter. Powers conferred by the Charter. Sailing of the Colonists. Arrival in the Chesapeake Bay. Landing on Blackiston Island. Settlement at St. Mary's. Friendly relations secured with the Indians. Extending the settlements to St. George's and Montgomery. Peace and Prosperity. Missionaries. A period of thirty years.*

SIR George Calvert, afterwards Lord Baltimore, an English gentleman of finished education, was the founder of Maryland. Being one of the principal Secretaries of State and a member of the House of Commons, he always maintained the rights and interests of the King, who, in consideration for this devotion, granted him a charter dated the 20th of June, 1632. The country granted by this charter was named Maryland, in honor of Queen Henrietta Maria.

Before the execution of this patent Lord Baltimore died, and his eldest son, Cecil, having inherited his father's title and estate, succeeded to the charter, he and his heirs, becoming absolute proprietors of Maryland. The Proprietary had full, free and absolute power to enact laws, with the advice, assent and approbation of the freemen of the province. The Proprietary had full power to grant to his colonists such tracts of land as they might purchase. He was also granted the license and faculty of erecting and founding churches, chapels and places of worship in convenient and suitable places, and of causing the land to be dedicated according to the laws of the Kingdom of England. The territories described by the charter extended from Watkins' Point, opposite the mouth of the Potomac River, northward to the fortieth degree of north latitude, and from the Atlantic Ocean and Delaware Bay on the east, to the Potomac River on the west. It will be seen that this included a part of what is now Pennsylvania and Delaware.

As soon as the grant was obtained, Cecil Calvert completed his arrangements for the establishment of a colony. Deeming that the interests of the enterprise demanded his remaining in England, he confided the colony to his brother, Leonard Calvert, whom he constituted Lieutenant General or Governor. The colony consisting of about two hundred persons embarked in two vessels, the Ark and the Dove, from the Isle of Wight on the 22nd of November, 1633. After many difficulties and some dangers, these two vessels, though separated by storms on the ocean, arrived safely off Point Comfort in Virginia, on the 24th of February, 1634. They landed on the 25th of March on an island, to which they gave the name of St. Clement's, now Blackiston's.

The colonists took solemn possession of Maryland with religious services conducted according to the usages of the Roman Catholic Church, and erected a cross as an emblem of Christianity and Civilization, which they were about to plant on these shores.

In order to make further discoveries, Governor Leonard Calvert proceeded up the Potomac, near to the place now called New Marlboro', where there was an Indian village governed by Archihu, uncle to the King, or Werowance, who was at that time an infant. When the Governor asked the Indian Chief if he were willing that his people should settle in this country, he replied, "I will not bid you go, neither will I bid you stay, but you may use your own discretion." Using this discretion, the Governor concluded it was not safe to settle so high up the river. He explored the St. George, a small river on the north side of the Potomac, and about twelve miles from the mouth, anchored at the village of the Yoacomico Indians. The Governor explained to the Chief, or Werowance, his object in coming to his country. The Werowance, after the custom of the Indians, made but little answer to the proposition of Governor Calvert; but, nevertheless, hospitably entertained him and his companions, giving up his own rude bed for the accommodation of the Governor.

Having carefully examined the surrounding country, and finding it possessed of many advantages which rendered it an eligible site, Calvert determined to commence at this place, his first settlement. The ship and pinnace which he had left at St.

Clement's were ordered to join him at Yoacomico. To prepare the way for a peaceable admission into the country, he presented the Werowance and principal men with clothes, axes, hoes and knives; in return for which they granted him about thirty miles of territory, which he called Augusta Carolina, afterwards the County of St. Mary's. The character of these presents to the Werowance indicates the desire of the colonists to introduce among the savages the first rudiments, as it were, of civilization—the implements of agriculture.

The Indians agreed to give up one-half of their village for the immediate accommodation of the settlers, including one-half of their corn grounds, which they had already commenced to plant. Upon the 27th day of March, 1634, the Governor took possession of the place and named the town St. Mary's.

The Indians lived in the greatest harmony with the settlers, they hunted together for deer and turkeys, while the women and children became domesticated in the families of the English. The principles of Christianity and philanthropy always governed the colonists in their treatment of the savages. Earnest and persistent efforts were made to teach them religious truth and the arts of civilized life, while their territorial and personal rights were scrupulously respected. The rights of the aborigines were purchased for a consideration which gave them satisfaction. While no rewards were offered for Indian scalps, they gave them words and acts of love and mercy.

The relations that existed between the natives and the settlers continued to be friendly until William Clayborne, called by historians the Evil Genius of the colony, excited the fears and jealousies of the Indians, by persuading them that the new comers were not English, but Spaniards, the enemies of the English. The simple natives believed him and suddenly withdrew from St. Mary's.

The settlers fearing a hostile attack, postponed the building of their own houses, and erected a block-house or fortification, regulating their conduct in the meantime towards the savages, so as to re-awaken the old feelings of confidence and intimacy. The natives became convinced of the falsehood of the insinuations against the settlers, and again resorted to the colony. The land was divided among the settlers under the instructions of the Proprietary. Owing to the dangers both from the savages and their own countrymen from Kent Island and Virginia, the colonists were not disposed to extend their settlements beyond the limits of St. Mary's. Lots of five and ten acres, within the city, were granted to all who might apply for them, while tracts ranging from one hundred to three thousand acres were granted to those persons applying. A rent of twenty shillings for every thousand acres was reserved for the Proprietary.

The settlements continued to grow and prosper; already the plantations had extended to the west side of St. George's River, and large accessions were being added from the northern country. New hundreds—or divisions similar to our election districts—were erected.

The two missionaries who accompanied the colony confined their efforts to converting the Indians who were friendly with the settlers. As the colony increased new missionaries arrived from England, and immediately began to penetrate into the interior and visit every tribe and village. The Indians at Patuxent received them very kindly and bestowed upon them a plantation called St. Mattopany on the Patuxent, where a missionary station and store house were immediately erected. Three men travelled in a boat, subsisted by hunting, and at night slept under cover of a slight tent. In five years they had extended them throughout the greater part of the province. They visited many tribes and made many converts. They had four permanent stations, the most distant of which was one hundred and fifty miles, located on the Monocacy River, near where the City of Frederick now stands. Another was on the Patuxent River, near where Triadelphia is located.

The conversion and baptism of Tayac, the chief of the Piscataways, the most extensive and powerful tribe in Maryland, was the cause of considerable rejoicing among the colonists. The chief was taken violently sick, and the forty medicine men that surrounded him failed with all their arts of conjuring to cure him, one of the missionaries obtained permission to treat him and soon restored him to health.

Tayac after this abandoned the habits and dress of the savage and adopted that of the English, and learned their language. What is Prince George's County now was rapidly settled, emigrants moving up the Potomac and Patuxent Rivers.

Frederick County embraced all that section of country lying west of a line drawn from the mouth of Rock Creek to the Patuxent River, which had formerly been embraced within the limits of Prince George's. Thus it will be seen that what now constitutes Montgomery County belonged to Frederick County in the early settlement of the colonies. The earliest settlement within the limits of Montgomery commenced in the year 1650, by Robert Brooke, who founded a Protestant settlement of forty persons, including his wife and ten children, at Della Brooke on the Patuxent River. During the next thirty years peace and prosperity reigned throughout the province. Persons of wealth and distinction sought the new world for enlarged and unoccupied fields in which to employ their wealth and talents, while those who were proscribed for their political or religious opinions, were eager to abandon the shores of their native land and seek homes in this, the Eldorado of the West.

When it is remembered that steamships were then unknown, with no submarine cable to flash along its electric wire the intelligence of weal or woe to friends at home, and an equally wild and trackless wilderness before them, the abode of wild beasts and savage men, is it not indeed wonderful to contemplate the progress of settlement in the American colonies? Still, amid all these dangers and difficulties, they subdued the wilderness, founded communities, erected town and cities, and in a little more than two hundred years, have founded an Empire that wields a sceptre equal to the combined powers of the East.

# CHAPTER IV.

*Climate and Productions. Tobacco and Corn, staple productions. Oysters, Game and Fish. Indentured Whites. Slaves introduced from Virginia. Tobacco the medium of barter and exchange. Tobacco shipments. Silver coins. Fruit and Cider. Mails. Quakers or Friends. Indians. Toleration.*

THE climate and beneficent laws that governed the colony of Maryland continued to attract immigration, and the number of counties continued to increase. They speedily made clearings in the forest, and reduced the land to cultivation. Tobacco and corn were the principal articles cultivated. Great attention was paid to fruit;—while the waters of the bay and rivers furnished the greatest of delicacies, oysters, wild ducks and fish. The people were planters and farmers, and there were no influences to draw the people together, like in towns and cities, but left the people free to lay the foundation of that peculiar domestic life which has always been the characteristic and charm of Maryland. Slavery was introduced from Virginia, and superseded the white servants that were so frequently to be found in the early days of the colony. These were white emigrants, who, wanting the means to emigrate, apprenticed their time, for a certain period, to those who would bear that expense. This was made a matter of barter. Usually the captain of a ship would bring out a party of emigrants, taking an indenture from the emigrant, instead of passage money, for which he agreed to serve for a given time. On the arrival of the ships with such emigrants, their unexpired time was sold to the highest bidder; the price was paid in tobacco, which was at that time the currency of the province. The cultivation of tobacco claimed the attention of almost every one; it was the great bonanza of the times, and hundreds of ships were employed in its transportation abroad. There was no money in general use at this time, and trade was conducted through the medium of barter, or the exchange of one commodity for another.  In 1650, silver coins were issued by the Proprietary, of various denominations, having Lord Baltimore's arms on one side, while on the other was the motto, *Crescite et Multiplicamini*.  Very little of this coin came into general circulation; tobacco had become the common currency of the province—one pound of it being equal to three pence English money.  It was made a legal tender, at one penny a pound, in 1732.

The luxuries of the present day were unknown; they sat upon stones and benches; the back of the bench was so constructed that it could be turned up, and form the top for a table, around which sat the hardy pioneers, after the toils and excitements of the day, consequent upon the life of a frontiersman, drank their cider and sack, in lieu of coffee and tea, which were seldom used.  Apples and peaches were raised in great abundance; two or three varieties of white apples were cultivated for summer use, while long stem, red, red streak, and black red streak were the principal varieties in use for autumn and winter.

Communication was had, in the absence of post roads and mail facilities, by sending letters through private hands, and it is astonishing with what rapidity a letter or communication would travel through these sparsely settled communities.  Each and every one of the settlers were alike interested in the prompt and safe delivery of the letters intrusted to their care to forward, and would often leave their work and mount the fastest horse on the plantation, and speed to the next settlement, where it would again be taken in charge, and in a like manner forwarded to the next settlement or plantation, and so on until it reached the person for whom it was directed; in this way letters travelled fifty and sixty miles in the course of twenty-four hours, rivalling, in point of time, the delivery by some of the local mails at the present time.

Travelling was done on horseback by land, while canoes or small boats were brought into requisition when it was desirable or expedient to travel by water.

The Quakers, or Friends as they are called, found in this province a refuge and home from their persecutors.  In the province of Massachusetts, laws had been passed that proscribed them as a " *Cursed Sect.*"  They were imprisoned " without bail," and sentenced to banishment upon " pain of death."

They were to be maimed, whipped, and "men or women to have their tongues bored through with a red hot iron." These persecutions led George Fox, a zealous leader, to come to Maryland; being delighted with the country and realizing the fact, that the laws and liberal policy of the province placed no restrictions upon religious liberty, he remained in the colony and preached the doctrines of his sect, both to the settlers and the natives, Indian chiefs and their subjects. The members of the Legislature and the Council, men of distinction, justices of the peace, and even the heir of the Proprietary himself came to listen to him preach. Maryland was indeed, to the Friends, the *Land of Promise.* Whatever difficulties they may have had with the government came from refusal to perform military duty, and their rejection of oaths; but they were subsequently relieved even of these requirements. They established settlements or meetings through St. George's and Montgomery Counties, and accomplished a great deal towards promoting the material development and intellectual advancement of the country. The first house built by the Friends in Montgomery County, was by James Brooke, on "Brooke Grove," granted in 1728. Here Friends gathered in sufficient numbers to establish a flourishing meeting, and, a little more than a century ago, they took a step that distinguished them from surrounding communities, by the emancipation of their slaves. The house is occupied at present by William J. Schofield. By their patient industry and perseverance, combined with their intellectual culture, social intercourse, agricultural knowledge, their fidelity to the principles of moral truth and human advancement, the Quakers have left an impress upon the character of the whole people, which has given an emulating stimulus to their aims and energies, which will be in powerful and unabated operation, when the marble and bronze, that now commemorates less meritorious achievements, shall have disappeared under the corroding influences of the march of time.

During this time the aborigines and the colonists were living side by side upon terms of the greatest friendship.

The Chesapeakes had disappeared entirely from Maryland, and the remnant of the tribe had removed to the banks of the Elizabeth River, in Virginia, under the protection and dominion of the Powhatans. The Yoacomicos still lived upon the St.

3

Mary's River, and had become mostly domesticated with the settlers. The Susquehannocks, at the head of the Chesapeake Bay, who were at some distance from the colonists, and less under the influence of the whites than the Yoacomicos, with whom they were at enmity, and constantly at war, gave the settlers some trouble; but as the pioneers were constantly pushing their discoveries and explorations northward and westward, and as the stream of emigration continued to pour into the colony from all parts of Europe, but more especially the English, Scotch and Welsh, the Indians were compelled to withdraw from the homes of their fathers, and seek new hunting grounds towards the setting sun.

The Piscataways and Anacostians, under the fostering care of the settlers, and the wise and beneficent teachings of the missionaries, were fast becoming civilized and adopting the habits of the whites. Their ideas of civilization seemed to centre in the possession of a hat. When once the Indian consented to wear a hat, it was *prima facie* evidence that the Indian heart had been changed, and his savage instincts converted from the war-path and the chase, to those of a more modern and civilized character. Among the numerous cases of the Indians' friendship towards the first settlers, the following incident will illustrate the friendly feelings existing among the Piscataways for the whites. Madam Perrie, her three sons and son-in-law left Europe in 1695, and commenced a settlement on the Patuxent River, near where Magruder's Ferry is now located. As they were journeying along on the evening of a summer's day, they reached the verge of a hill commanding a view of the valley of the Potomac. It was a beautiful woodland scene; a vast forest stretching along as far as the eye could reach, inhabited by wild beasts and birds of prey. No indication of civilized man was anywhere near; scattered along the banks of the river, amidst the dark green hazel, could be discovered the Indian wigwams, the smoke issuing therefrom in its spiral form. No sound was heard but the songs of the birds; in silence they contemplated the beautiful prospect which nature presented to their view. Suddenly a number of Indians darted from the woods—the females shrieked—when an Indian advanced, and, in broken English, said to Madame Perrie, "Indian no harm white—white good to Indian—go to Mattawoma—our chief—come to Mattawoma." Few were the words of the Indian. They went with him to Mattawoma's cabin; and Mattawoma, with the humanity that distinguished the Indians of that tribe, gave up to the immigrants his wigwam. The next day he conveyed them to the Indian village of Piscataway, which was fifteen miles below, where now stands Washington, and at the mouth of Piscataway Creek, where resided their Chief, Tayac, to whom he introduced the madame and her retinue. The chief entertained them in regal style and splendor, and gave them permission to settle in any portion of his dominions. During the entire subsequent history of the province, no aggressive war was ever waged by her people against the Indians. They dwelt together in peace and amity, until the latter either emigrated to the West, or lost their identity as a people by absorption. Some unimportant conflicts took place with the Indians during the progress of the settlements. These were principally to repel the inroads of hostile tribes from beyond her borders, but none could be dignified as wars.

Such consideration had our forefathers for the rights of these people, that when the Senecas, a tribe of the Six Nations, who came from the State of New York, invaded their territory, under a claim of doubtful right to a portion of its soil, instead of repulsing the hostile incursion and driving them back to their homes, they appointed commissioners to settle the dispute, and purchased their alleged claim for three hundred pounds sterling. The colony having respected the rights of the original owners of the soil, exercised the same justice and forbearance towards their European brethren, who came and settled among them.

Although religious toleration had been declared by the Proprietary as one of the fundamental principles of the social union over which he presided; yet, in order to give the principle the sanction of authority, the Assembly proceeded to incorporate it in the laws of the province. It was enacted, that no person, professing to believe in Jesus Christ, should be molested in respect to his religion, or the free exercise thereof; and that any one who should reproach his neighbor with opprobrious names, of religious distinction, should pay a fine to the person insulted. Thus it will be seen that Maryland was the first province in which religious toleration was established by law. While at this very period the Puritans were persecuting their Protestant brethren in New England, and the Episcopalians were retorting with the same severity on the Puritans in Virginia, there was forming, in Maryland, a sanctuary where all might worship, and none might oppress; and where even Protestants sought refuge from Protestant intolerance.

Annapolis, which had been erected into a port of entry in 1683, was made the seat of government in 1691. For a period of forty years the colony enjoyed almost undisturbed tranquillity. The only troubles were contests between the Governor and Council, who formed the upper house, and the delegates of the people in the lower house. These struggles were the germ of that mighty contest in which the liberties of the people were finally secured.

# CHAPTER V.

## LAND GRANTS.

THE general progress of settlement in what is now Montgomery County, was to the north and westward, a course which has uniformly been pursued in every State and community since the earliest history. Among the first of recorded patents is that of

**Joseph's Park,** and was granted to William Joseph, May 20th, 1689, containing four thousand two hundred and twenty acres. This tract lies on the east side of Rock Creek and embraces Knowles' Station, Forest Glen Station and Linden Station, including the farms of Alfred Ray, William A. Batchelor, and Carroll's or St. John's Chapel. The Brookville and Washington Turnpike passes through it, from Augustus Burgdorf's farm nearly to Grace Church.

**Girl's Portion.** This was surveyed for Colonel Henry Dulaney, in 1688. Extends from Rock Creek, eastward, to O. H. P. Clark's farm, three and three-eighths miles. The Ashton and Sligo Turnpike passes through the tract. The Silver Spring Farm, the estate of the late F. P. Blair, and the residence of the Hon. Montgomery Blair, includes a portion of the tract; also, the Silver Spring Station and Sligo. The Brookville and Washington Turnpike crosses it.

**Leeke Forest.** This additional tract of seven hundred and ten acres, was also surveyed for Colonel Henry Dulaney, in 1688. It lies west of "Joseph's Park," on the west side of Rock Creek, and extends west one and seven-eighths miles. The Rockville and Georgetown Turnpike passes through it. The farms of the late Samuel Perry and William Hudleston, on the old Georgetown road, and Bethesda Church are included within its limits.

**Hermitage.** Granted to William Joseph, May 2nd, 1689, for three thousand eight hundred and sixty-six acres. This grant lies on the east side of Rock Creek and adjoins "Joseph's Park" on the north, and extending from Vier's Mill to the intersection of the Rockville and Washington Turnpike with the Union Turnpike Company's road. The Brookville and Washington Turnpike passes through it from the Watery Branch to one-fourth of a mile south of Mitchell's Cross Roads. The City road, from Rockville to Washington passes through it, from Graves' farm to Aug. Burgdorf's farm, at the intersection of the Brookville and Washington Turnpike. The Norwood Turnpike traverses the tract from Kemp's store to Lyddane's farm, or its intersection with the Brookville and Washington Turnpike. It embraces many fine farms and elegant residences. Lying to the east of "Hermitage" is

**St. Winexburg,** surveyed for John Woodcock, May 3rd, 1689, for five hundred acres, extending from the North-west branch at Kemp's Mill, westward one and one-half miles west of the Brookville and Washington Turnpike. The road from Kemp's Mill to Lyddane's farm and the Norwood Turnpike passes through it. This grant includes the estate of the late William Pierce. Immediately north of "St. Winexburg" is located

**Carroll's Forest,** granted to Charles Carroll, May 3rd, 1689, consisting of five hundred acres. This tract was conveyed May 3rd, 1794, by Charles Carroll, of Carrollton, to John Connelly. On the west side of Rock Creek, north of "Leeke Forest," and west of "Hermitage," is a tract called

**Dan,** granted Thomas Brooke, September 6th, 1694, for three thousand six hundred and ninety-seven acres, extending from Rock Creek, one and a half miles west, and up the creek north, two and seven-eighths of a mile. The Georgetown Turnpike

passes over it from Mr. Codwise's farm to that of the late
Samuel Perry.  The year following, attracted no doubt by the
fertility of the bottom lands lying on the banks of the Potomac,
Richard Brightwell, with a more adventurous spirit than any
of the previous settlers, and actuated by a noble impulse,
ascended the Potomac River above the mouth of the Great
Seneca, and sought to establish a settlement far from his neighbors, where he and his friends could enjoy the pleasure and
excitements of fishing and hunting.  Here could be found in
abundance, buffaloes, bears, wolves and deer; the Sugar Loaf
Mountain and the chain of hills that extend to the Monocacy
River, affording them ample shelter and protection from the
skill and pursuit of the wily hunter.  He located his grant
between Edward's Ferry and the mouth of the Great Seneca,
and named it

**Brightwell's Hunting Quarter,** patented August 29th,
1695, and contained one thousand and eighty-six acres.  It extended for about four miles along the Potomac River, and is
now traversed its entire length by the Chesapeake and Ohio
Canal.  The beginning of this tract was destroyed in the construction of the canal, but a suitable stone was planted in its
stead at the bottom of the canal, which is known only to a few
persons.  Leaving Mr. Brightwell with his dogs and guns, to
enjoy himself to the best of his ability, for the next twenty-
five years the course of settlements on Rock Creek, continued
west of the Creek.  Located west of "Joseph's Park," and
south of "Leeke Forest," is situated

**Clean Drinking,** patented to John Coats, October 1st,
1699, for seven hundred acres.  This tract extends down Rock
Creek to Jones' Bridge.  Walter C. Jones established a mill on
this survey, and leaves his epitaph upon an old stone that still
remains a living monument of his folly.  The inscription, though
somewhat defaced by time, is still legible, it reads:

" Here lies the body and bones
Of old Walter C. Jones;
By his not thinking,
He lost ' Clean Drinking,'
And by his shallow pate,
He lost his vast estate."

Following the settlements on Rock Creek, comes those upon the Patuxent River.

**Bear Neck,** granted Benjamin Williams, March 26th, 1700, for one hundred and fifty acres. Adjacent to this, and lying to the south, is

**Maiden's Fancy,** to Neal Clark, surveyed September 11th, 1700, for five hundred and eighty acres. This tract is situated in the south-east corner of the County, and the intersection of the Patuxent. Two miles above on the river, is

**Bear Bacon,** surveyed for Mark Richardson, June 24th, 1703, containing six hundred acres. The Ashton and Laurel road passes through this tract from the cemetery to Liberty Grove school-house. The next settlements made in the County were located in the south-western part, between Rock Creek and the Potomac River.

**Friendship,** patented to Thomas Addison and James Stoddart, December 1st, 1711, for three thousand one hundred and twenty-four acres. This land extends from near the Potomac and below Edmund Brooke's farm, a south-easterly and easterly direction across the Georgetown Turnpike, north of Tenallytown, and up the pike, north-westerly, near to Bethesda post office, and contains many rich and valuable farms; Allison Nailor's lands, and the farms of Richard Williams, Henry Loughborough, and others. The river road passes through from Rider's farm to near Tenallytown. Adjoining, and on the east, lies

**Charles and Thomas,** surveyed for Charles Beale and Thomas Fletchall, April 8th, 1715, containing four hundred and nineteen acres. The road from Tenallytown to Jones' Bridge, runs through the land. On the north, and west of "Friendship," lies another tract, called

**Friendship,** *for Thomas Beale and Charles Fletchall,* May 2nd, 1715, for one thousand three hundred and sixty-eight acres. This tract extends from the farms of L. A. Lodge, in a north-east course as far as C. W. Lansdale's farm.

**Clagett's Purchase,** surveyed for Thomas Fletchall, April 10th, 1715, containing seven hundred and seventy-two acres, and situated west of "Clean Drinking," and south of "Leeke Forest." The Georgetown Turnpike crosses the tract from the branch below Bethesda Church, to nearly its intersection with the old Georgetown road. Immediately west of this, is

**Huntington,** surveyed for Thomas Fletchall, December 10th, 1715, comprising three hundred and seven acres. It is divided by the old Georgetown road. West of "Leeke Forest," and west of "Huntington," comes

**Contention,** granted to William Fitz Redmau, February 5th, 1715, containing six hundred and twenty acres, embracing the farms of Mr. Yeabower, and others. North of "Hermitage" and east of Rock Creek, is found

**Bradford's Rest,** granted to Major John Bradford, June 3rd, 1713, comprising two thousand six hundred and fifty-eight acres. Adjacent, and on the west, lies the

**Addition to Bradford's Rest,** granted to Major John Bradford, September 20th, 1715, for five hundred and eighty-four acres. And again, the same lands re-surveyed, with lands added, and called

**Bradford's Rest,** for Major John Bradford, June 10th, 1718, containing four thousand eight hundred and ninety-two acres. This tract extends up Rock Creek, north, as far as William E. Muncaster's farm, and east, as far as the late Roger Brooke's farm. The road from Rockville to Baltimore runs through the grant, from William S. Brooke's farm to Granville Stabler's farm, three and one-half miles; and the Brookville and Washington Turnpike runs through it from near Higgins' Tavern, nearly to Ranies' store, The lands embrace many elegant farms, including those of Philip Riley, Charles Abert, the late Roger Brooke, A. R. Wadsworth, William S. Brooke, Hon. Allen Bowie Davis, A. H. Herr, and others.

The streams and water courses seem to have attracted the attention of the early settlers, as is proven by the location of the grants. First comes Rock Creek, and then North-West branch which was the next point selected by the emigrants, followed by the settlements along the Patuxent; after this come Watts' Branch and Hawling's River. The first on Watts' Branch, was

**Dung Hill,** surveyed for Walter Evans, August 10th, 1715, containing five hundred and thirty-six acres. It was situated on the Potomac, at the mouth of Watts' Branch. The Chesapeake and Ohio Canal runs through it, as does also the river road, from near Watts' Branch to Cornell's farm.  Immediately below this grant, lying along the Potomac, comes

**Thompson's Hop Yard,** patented by John Thompson, December 8th, 1715, and which embraced one hundred acres. This is but a short distance above the Great Falls.

**Cool Spring Level,** to Archibald Edmonston, April 28th, 1717, containing five hundred and ninety-two acres. This tract is situated on the road from Offutt's Cross Roads to the Great Falls.  On the north of this road,

**Allison's Park,** surveyed for John Allison, June 10th, 1715, embracing six hundred and twenty acres, and lying south of Watts' Branch.  Adjacent to this,

**Archibald's Lot,** granted to James Moore, March 17th, 1718.  This tract lies on the road from Rockville to the Great Falls, and contained one hundred acres, and is embraced in the farm of Jacob Miller.

**Younger Brother.**  This tract lies west of Watts' Branch, and was surveyed for William Offutt, August 21st, 1717, and contained six hundred acres, and comprises the farms of William Viers and Joseph T. Bailey.  Following this, comes

**Dispute,** lying on the head-waters of Watts' Branch, surveyed for Charles and William Beall, January 19th, 1719, containing six hundred and seventy acres.  An older tract then lies to the east of this, and is called the

**Two Brothers,** comprising twelve hundred acres, through which passes Watts' Branch and the road from Rockville to Darnestown.  The next that claims attention on Watts' Branch, is

**The Exchange,** for Arthur Nelson, granted March 10th, 1718, for four hundred and eighteen acres; and again, to the same person, January 28th, 1719,

**The New Exchange,** for one hundred and fifty acres. These two were re-surveyed, December 20th, 1721, and were called "Exchange and New Exchange Enlarged," for Arthur Nelson, and contained sixteen hundred and twenty acres.  By this extension the tract extended down Watts' Branch a long distance, and embraced the site upon which Rockville was originally built.  The road from Rockville to the Great Falls passes for more than two miles through the tract.  The County Poor House farm, Judge Bouic's, (O'Neal's,) John E. Wilson's, and other farms are included in this tract. North of "Dan," mentioned previous, is the

**Addition to Dan,** surveyed for Philip Lee, December 10th, 1717, containing five hundred and seventy-six acres; traversed by the Georgetown Turnpike. Then came Joseph West and James Holmard, who joined in a co-partnership, and had a tract surveyed, containing five hundred and thirty-five acres, and when they came to give it a name, were at considerable trouble to select one that would give satisfaction to both partners, each wanted his name selected for the tract, so as to appear on the records at Annapolis. Much was said on the subject by both parties; finally a compromise was effected by mutual friends, who taking their two Christian names, joined them with the copulative conjunction "and," which gave them

**Joseph and James,** and was so patented October 15th, 1718. It is situated on the road from Rockville to Gaithersburg, and embraces the farms of Samuel Clements and others.

# CHAPTER VI.

## LAND GRANTS—CONTINUED.

*Easy Purchase. Friendship Enlarged. Drumaldry. Lay Hill. Snowden's Manor. Snowden's Manor Enlarged. Charles and Benjamin. George the Third. Beall's Manor. Beall Christie. Bear Garden Enlarged. Deer Park. Snowden Mill. Charley Forest. Addition to Charley Forest. Hygham. Gold's Branch. Gitting's Hah! Hah!! Bordley's Choice. Brooke Grove. Addition to Brooke Grove. John and Sarah. Benjamin's Lot. New Year's Gift. Autra. Easy Come By. Mill Land. Boyd's Delay. Magruder's Hazard. Paradise. Bernard's Desire. Wickham and Pottinger's Discovery. Partnership. The Brother' Industry. Deer Park. Fellowship. Constant Friendship.*

IN following the succession of settlements, it is necessary to return to the North-west Branch, where Archibald Edmonston found an

**Easy Purchase,** granted April 23rd, 1716, consisting of nine hundred acres, extending from the North-west Branch to the West Point Branch. The Ashton and Sligo Turnpike runs through the entire length of it, from John T. Baker's farm below and near Colesville, to the late Johns Hopkins farm at the intersection of the Columbia road. Crossing to the east side of the North-west Branch, is located

**Friendship Enlarged,** for Alexander Beall, May 14th, 1716, containing nine hundred and twenty acres, and extending from near the County line up to the north of Bond's Mill, on the Ashton and Sligo Turnpike. A short distance north of "Carroll's Forest," heretofore described, lies a tract called

**Drumaldry,** surveyed for James Beall, September 16th, 1715, for two hundred and twenty-five acres. It lies on the North-west Branch and embraces the farm of James Bonifant. On the North-west Branch, and still north of this, James Beall was granted

**Lay Hill,** August 17th, 1716, containing one thousand two hundred and ninety-eight acres.  The North-west Branch runs through the tract, while the Norwood Turnpike passes the entire length.  The farms of Abraham Van Horn, A. J. Cashell and others are situated on it.  On the ridge dividing the head waters of the Patuxent River and North-west Branch, lies a tract embracing many farms called

**Snowden's Manor,** surveyed for Richard Snowden, December 10th, 1715, containing one thousand acres.  The Ashton and Sligo Turnpike runs through the estate, also the road from Ashton to Laurel.  The tract embraces the lands of William John Thomas, the farms of William Lee, Warwick Miller, Asa Stabler, and the farm and bone mill of William Bond.  A re-survey was made twenty-eight years after and was called

**Snowden's Manor Enlarged,** for Richard Snowden, dated March 5th, 1743, and embraced nine thousand two hundred and sixty-five acres.  This Manor contains some of the finest farms in the County.  The Laurel road passes through it from Ashton, through Spencerville to the cemetery near Liberty Grove Church.  The turnpike from Ashton to Winpenny's farm near Colesville runs upon it, while the Norwood Turnpike passes through it from Joseph Moore's farm to Van Horn's farm.  The North-west Branch runs through the tract from near Ashton to Kemp's Mill.

**Charles and Benjamin,** surveyed and granted to Charles Beall, July 2nd, 1718, containing two thousand two hundred and eighty acres.  This tract extends from E. J. Hall's farm down the Brookville and Washington Turnpike to Higgins' Tavern, embracing the farms of Z. D. Waters, Thomas Waters, Josiah W. Jones, Samuel Cashell, and others.  The Episcopal Church at Mechanicsville is located on this grant.  The town of Mechanicsville is built on a small tract occasioned by a vacancy between older surveys, and was named after the King of England,

**George the Third,** and granted to Richard Brooke, July 28th, 1763, and contained forty-seven acres.  Returning again to West Point Branch,

**Beall's Manor** is found, granted to Charles and William Beall, February 14th, 1720, embracing seventeen hundred and eighty-seven acres.  Situated on the head-waters of West Point

Branch, beginning in Thomas Winpenny's house-yard, a mile north of Colesville on the Ashton and Sligo Turnpike. On it are located the farms of Thomas Winpenny, Mr. O'Hare, Lloyd Green, J. W. Bancroft, and others. Colesville stands on a tract adjacent to "Beall's Manor," surveyed about the same time, and called **Beall Christie,** and contained five hundred and six acres. Colesville is a thriving village of recent date.

**Bear Garden Enlarged,** surveyed for Archibald Edmonston, November 10th, 1716, containing twelve hundred and sixty-five acres. Adjoining this tract,

**Deer Park,** surveyed for Archibald Edmonston, February 14th, 1720, containing six hundred and eighty-two acres. This grant, including "Beall Christie," lies between the West Point and the East Point Branches, and embrace the farms of Julius Marlow, and others. Adjacent to " Beall's Manor," is

**Snowden Mill,** granted to Richard Snowden in October, 1723, surveyed for five hundred and forty-six acres. The Columbia road passes by this tract; while it is well watered by the West Point Branch passing through it. Nancy Brown's farm, and others are included, as also the road from John Leizar's to Nancy Brown's.

**Charley Forest,** was granted to Major John Bradford, and contained one thousand two hundred and thirty acres. Increased by

**Addition to Charley Forest,** surveyed for the same person, September 16th, 1720. These two united, extend from Mechanicsville to within a short distance of where Snell's Bridge crosses the Patuxent River. The turnpike from Mechanicsville to Sandy Springs and Ashton passes over it, and from Ashton, the road to Snell's Bridge; and the road to Brighton runs on it. On this tract is situated Sandy Springs and Ashton, including many valuable farms, viz: Fair Hill farm, at Mechanicsville, with the farms of William H. Farquhar, Albin Gilpin, R. T. Bentley, Edward Thomas, and many others. The tract is located on the dividing ridge that separates the head-waters of the North-west Branch and Cabin Creek.

In following the order of dates in settlement, Hawlings' River is reached, when

**Hygham** is found, granted to John Bradford, February 23rd, 1720, surveyed for one hundred acres. Beginning from the same tree, is

**Gold's Branch,** granted to Richard Snowden, July 30th, 1722, for two hundred and fifty-seven acres. These two grants lie on Hawlings' River, and constituted a portion of the farm of Hon. Allen Bowie Davis, his residence being located on the latter, through which the Westminster road passes, and also Gold Branch, a small tributary of Hawlings' River.

**Gitting's Hah! Hah!!** was surveyed for Thomas Spriggs and Richard Simmons, July 27th, 1724, and contained five hundred and seventeen acres, lying on both sides of Hawlings' River, embracing the following farms: James T. Holland's, Thomas John Holland's, William Brown's, and others. Adjoining this, lies

**Bordley's Choice,** granted to Thomas Bordley, April 8th, 1725, for one thousand acres. The Reedy Branch, an off-shoot of Hawlings' River, divides the tract and affords plenty of water to the following farms: Thomas J. Holland's, William Riggs', Thomas Riggs' and Brice Howard's. The Brookville Academy is located on this survey. Adjoining this grant lies a tract, originally

**Brooke Grove,** surveyed for James Brooke, September 4th, 1728, and a re-survey for the same person, November 15th, 1741, for three thousand one hundred and fifty-four acres, and again re-surveyed, so as to include the adjacent vacancies, and named

**Addition to Brooke Grove,** surveyed for James Brooke, September 29th, 1762, and contained seven thousand nine hundred and six acres. After this addition to his Grove, he had eleven thousand and sixty acres granted by patent, and six thousand by purchase, and owned at the time of his death, nearly twenty thousand acres.

This tract extends from Thomas J. Holland's farm, some eight or nine miles in a north-westerly direction, beyond the Big Seneca. The town of Brookeville, which was founded in 1780, and Laytonsville are situated on it. The road from Brookeville to Laytonsville passes through the tract, which embraces some of the finest farms in the County, including those of E. J. Hall, the late Dr. William B. Magruder, John Riggs, Charles Brooke, the late Walter Magruder, David L. Pugh, Thomas D. Gaither, and Samuel Riggs, of R. This was the largest tract of land owned by one person in the County, and gives an example of the wealth and influence enjoyed by these early Princes of the Manor. James Brooke was a descendant of Robert Brooke, who established a Protestant Colony at **Della Brooke,** on the Patuxent, on the 29th of June, 1650, seventy-eight years previous.

**John and Sarah,** surveyed for John Philburn, December 21st, 1724, and contained two hundred acres, includes the town of Unity.

**Benjamin's Lot,** surveyed for Benjamin Gaither, April 8th, 1725, for five hundred and sixteen acres. Located on the Patuxent River and embraces the town of Triadelphia, and includes the farms of Robert Brown, and others.

The Westminster road from Brookeville passes through "Bordley's Choice," "Gold Branch," "Addition to Brooke Grove" and "Benjamin's Lot," to the Patuxent Bridge.

**New Year's Gift,** granted to Thomas Bordley, October 11th, 1726, for eleven hundred and forty-three acres, and is situated near the head-waters of Hawlings' River. The road from Unity to Damascus runs through it. While it embraces the farms of the late Thomas Griffith, A. B. Worthington, Charles Hutton and Richard H. Griffith.

With the granting of this tract, the settlements along the Patuxent, Hawlings, and head-waters of the Big Seneca Rivers seemed to come to a close, and remained so until about 1741, when they again commenced, and rapidly continued until 1775, when very little vacant land remained.

Returning again to Rock Creek on the west side and passing down on the south of the road leading from Rockville to Baltimore, Caleb Litton has found a suitable place and concludes to look no farther, and

**Autra** is surveyed for him, January 18th, 1720, and found to contain four hundred and five acres; since which time, Hon. Allen Bowie Davis found it covenient to add a portion of this tract to his Rock Creek farm.

**Easy Come By,** surveyed for William Pottinger, and contained three hundred acres, granted to him October 2nd, 1722. Adjacent to this, is

**Mill Land,** surveyed for Edward Dawson, March 10th, 1724, contained two hundred and fourteen acres, and is situated on the west of Rock Creek, and lies on the north side of the road from Rockville to Baltimore, and embraces the farms of Judge Richard I. Bowie, and others. Three miles from Rockville, on the east of Rock Creek, and about one mile northeasterly from " Mill Land," lies

**Boyd's Delay,** surveyed November 12th, 1725, and granted to John Boyd, June 6th, 1727, and contained two hundred and thirty-three acres, afterwards increased by the addition of several tracts, both by purchase and grant. Many of his descendants are still to be found in the County. His great-grandson, the late Rev. R. T. Boyd, an eminent divine, and one of the founders of the Methodist Protestant Church, and father of the publisher of this volume, was born on this estate in 1794. His widow is still living and resides in Clarksburg of this County. The lands embrace the farms of William E. Muncaster, Roger B. Farquhar, and James F. Barnsly.

**Magruder's Hazard,** surveyed for Samuel and John Magruder, November 23rd, 1726, and contained one hundred acres.

**Paradise,** surveyed for Thomas Gittings, September 17th, 1728, for two hundred acres. These two tracts lie on the east side of Rock Creek. The road from Redland to Muncaster's Mill passes through them.

**Bernard's Desire,** surveyed for Luke Bernard, February 1st, 1723, containing two hundred and thirty acres. The road from Rockville to Redland passes through this tract, as also through the farm of the late John Bean.

**Wickham and Pottinger's Discovery,** surveyed for Nathan Wickham and Samuel Pottinger, January 1st, 1721, and contained one thousand acres, and is situated on Piney Branch, and embraces the farms of N. D. Offutt, Mary M. Dodd, Samuel Jones, and others.

**Partnership,** granted to Henry Massey and John Flint, April 4th, 1722, and comprised two hundred acres, and adjoins "Dung Hill," heretofore mentioned. Watts' Branch runs through the land, which embraces at present the farm of Elbert Perry.

**The Brothers' Industry,** surveyed for James Wallace, April 16th, 1722, for one thousand four hundred and twenty-
4

nine acres, and includes the farms of Edwin Wallace, Solon
Young, and others.

**Deer Park,** *surveyed for Ralph Crabb,* April 19th, 1722,
and contained four hundred and seventy acres. It lies on the
ridge separating the head-waters of Muddy Branch from those
of Whetstone Branch, and embraces a portion of Gaithersburg,
a station on the Metropolitan Railroad, and since its incorpora-
tion as a city, has rapidly improved.

**Fellowship,** surveyed for Nathan Wickham and Samuel
Pottinger, March 10th, 1723, and contained four hundred acres,
and lies on the head-waters of Whetstone Branch, and embraces
the farm of the late Charles Saffell and the late Nathan Cook's
home farm.

**Constant Friendship,** granted to Joseph West and James
Halmard in 1722, lies near Rockville, and includes the lands of
Levi Veirs, and others.

As an evidence of the rapid growth of the province of Maryland during those early colonial days, it is only necessary to
glance at the Records of the Counties, and by examining the
land patents, as described in this chapter, it will be found that
from the settlement of "Easy Purchase" in 1716, to the survey
of "Constant Friendship" in 1722, comprising as it does a large
portion of the County, was accomplished in the short space of
six years. And again, by examining the names and titles given
the various tracts, it will be found that our forefathers were
gentlemen of education and refinement—unlike the emigrant
of the present, who lands on our shores ignorant and penni-
less—they came to the New World to establish a country and
a home, where liberty of thought and freedom of speech were to
be the fundamental principles upon which to base their struc-
ture. They came and brought their wives, their children, and
their household gods, determined to brave all dangers, that
they might bequeath to their children an inheritance worthy of
their noble sires.

# CHAPTER VII.

## LAND GRANTS—CONTINUED.

*Wickham's Good Will. The Joseph. Middle Plantation. Magruder and Beall's Honesty. Clewerwald Enlarged. Goose Pond. Bear Den. Prevention. Saint Mary's. Valentine's Garden Enlarged. Re-survey on Valentine's Garden Enlarged. Haymond's Addition. Concord. Hanover. Flint's Grove. Happy Choice. Hopewell. Jeremiah's Park. Partnership. The Re-survey on Part of Forest. Bank's Venture. Abraham's Lot. Killmain. John's Delight. Conclusion. Turkey Thicket. Benjamin's Square. Spring Garden. Abel's Levels. Moore's Delight. Pork Plenty, if no Thieves. Chestnut Ridge. Ralfo. Grandmother's Good Will. Cow Pasture. Peach Tree Hill. Errors Corrected. Very Good. Bite the Biter. Silent Valley. Trouble Enough Indeed.*

IT will be seen that the first settlements, commencing in 1688, in Montgomery County, were along the banks of Rock Creek, extending up both banks of the stream as far as Rockville. Thence they sought the Patuxent, and continued to spread along the banks of this fertile stream as far as Snell's Bridge. Then the country lying west of Rock Creek, towards the Potomac, and north and east of Rockville, seems to have attracted the attention of the settlers. Next came the flat red lands along the Potomac, in the vicinity of Darnestown and Poolesville, which were surveyed and granted. Among the first was

**Wickham's Good Will,** surveyed for James Plummer in 1723, and contained two hundred and seventy acres. This tract is situated on Muddy Branch, near where the road from Gaithersburg to Du Fief's farm crosses the stream, and embraces the farm of J. Hardesty.

**The Joseph,** granted Joseph West, July 1st, 1723, and contained three hundred acres, lying on Muddy Branch. The road from Rockville to Darnestown passes through the tract, which has its beginning at a stone at the north-east corner of the bridge over Muddy Branch.

**Middle Plantation,** surveyed for Daniel Dulaney, May 30th, 1724, and embraced seven hundred and twenty-two acres. This tract is situated at the mouth of Great Seneca, where the Chesapeake and Ohio Canal passes through it.

**Magruder's and Beall's Honesty,** granted to Daniel Magruder and Charles Beall, May 16th, 1726, and contained one thousand seven hundred and twenty-six acres, extends from "*Leeke Forest*," described in a preceding chapter, in a south-westerly direction to the Potomac River, and down the river to Edmond Brooke's farm, then returns with, or parallel with "Friendship" and "Contention," before mentioned, and embraces the farm of William Reading. The Chesapeake and Ohio Canal passes through it.

**Clewerwald Enlarged,** surveyed for William Offutt, July 17th, 1728, contains two thousand acres, and embraces the farms of the late Philip Stone, George Bradley, Joshua W. Offutt, and others.

**Goose Pond,** surveyed for John Chittam, November 4th, 1726, for one hundred acres, lies on the Potomac a short distance above the Great Falls, and is traversed by the Chesapeake and Ohio Canal. Just below this, and immediately opposite the Great Falls, is

**Bear Den,** surveyed for William Offutt, April 4th, 1729, and contained two hundred acres.

**Prevention,** granted William Beall and others, July 4th, 1727, for eleven hundred and eighty-two acres. Rock Creek runs through the tract. Veirs' Mill is located at the crossing of the Rockville and Washington Road. It embraces the Rock Creek farm of Judge Bouic, and others.

**Saint Mary's,** granted Caleb Litton, June 28th, 1727, for sixty-seven acres, lies south of Rockville, on the city road. In a previous chapter it was stated that the original Rockville stood on "Exchange and New Exchange Enlarged." The additions will now be given:

**Valentine's Garden Enlarged,** surveyed for Arthur Nelson, June 17th, 1720, and contained nine hundred and fifty acres. The same re-surveyed as follows:

**Re-survey on Valentine's Garden Enlarged,** for Henry Wright Crabb, April 10th, 1753, for two thousand and eighty-five acres. On this tract stands the first addition to Rockville, and lies mostly north and north-west of Rockville, and extends as far as the Washington Grove Camp Ground.

**Haymond's Addition,** surveyed for John Haymond, November 10th, 1743, and contained three hundred acres. On this tract lies the second addition to Rockville, embracing that portion of the town recently laid out in the vicinity of the Metropolitan Railroad Depot and the Agricultural Fair Grounds.

About this time the tide of settlements slowly commenced to extend up the Potomac, and a neighbor is found for Richard Brightwell, who located near Edward's Ferry in 1695. For twenty-six years he had braved the perils of his "Hunting Quarter," and during this time had seldom visited the lower settlements, being content with his dogs, pet bears and deers for companions, until

**Concord** was granted to Daniel Dulaney, April 26th, 1721, for one thousand one hundred and six acres, which was located about one mile above "Brightwell's Hunting Quarter," on the Potomac River, and one hundred yards above the mouth of Broad Run, where the line begins and extends up the Potomac to some distance above White's Ferry, taking in most of the bottom lands, through which runs the Chesapeake and Ohio Canal.

**Hanover,** granted to Dr. Patrick Hepburn, March 16th, 1722, for one thousand five hundred acres. This tract is situated on the head-waters of the Dry Seneca, and embraces the farms of Howard Griffith, Samuel Darby, the late Grafton Beall, and others.

**Flint's Grove,** surveyed for John Flint, July 4th, 1722, and contained three hundred acres, lies on Dry Seneca, and includes the farm of Thomas Fife.

**Happy Choice,** surveyed for William Black, May 20th, 1724, for eleven hundred and eighty-six acres, and lies on the road from Barnesville to Rockville. William O. Sellman's farm and others are included in this tract.

**Hopewell,** granted to John Norress, October 31st, 1726, for three hundred acres, lies on the Little Monocacy, and is crossed by the road running from the mouth of Monocacy to Mount Ephraim, and is also joined by the farm of William Price.

**Jeremiah's Park,** surveyed for Jeremiah Hays, December 10th, 1747, and includes the site upon which Barnesville stands. Sellman's Station and Post Office, one mile from Barnesville on the Metropolitan Railroad, also called Barnesville Station, are located on this tract.

**Partnership,** surveyed for Charles Diggs and John Bradford, April 16th, 1728, for two thousand acres, lies on Dry Seneca, and embraces the farms of Thomas Darby, Robert H. C. Allnutt, Samuel Dyson, F. S. Poole, John T. Fletchall, and others.

**The Re-survey on Part of Forest,** surveyed for Robert Peter, May 17th, 1784, containing one thousand seven hundred and ninety-six and one-fourth acres, embraces the lands in and around Poolesville. The first house in which was built by John Poole, in 1793.

**Banks' Venture,** surveyed for John Banks, November 29th, 1752, and contained one hundred acres, includes the present site of Redland.

**Abraham's Lot,** granted Cornelius Etting in 1732, on the Potomac River, near the mouth of Broad Run.

**Killmain,** granted to Daniel Carroll in 1735, and contains three thousand acres, lies on the Conrad's Ferry road, and includes the lands of Ludowick Young's heirs, and others.

**John's Delight,** granted and surveyed for John Harriss, June 14th, 1755, embraces the lands in and adjacent to Martinsburg and Conrad's Ferry.

**Conclusion,** granted Daniel Dulauey in 1731, embraces the farms of Joseph Dawson, Frederick Dawson, Col. George W. Dawson, and others,—all finely improved.

**Turkey Thicket,** granted and surveyed for John Magruder, September, 1736, and embraces the farms of Zadok Magruder, and others.

**Benjamin's Square,** granted Benjamin Wallingford in 1743, includes the farms adjacent to Goshen.

**Spring Garden,** granted Higison Belt in 1738, includes the farm of James Williams, and the lands near Laytonsville.

**Abel's Levels,** granted to Abel Brown in 1741, and

**Moore's Delight,** granted to Benjamin Penn in 1748, lies on the head-waters of the Great Seneca Creek, and embraces the farms of Col. Lyde Griffith, and others.

**Pork Plenty, if no Thieves,** granted to Nathan Ward in 1753, lies on the Patuxent, and embraces the lands in and around Duvall's Old Mill.

**Chestnut Ridge,** granted to George Buchanan in 1732, embraced the lands in and adjacent to Germantown Station, on the Metropolitan Railroad.

**Ralfo,** granted George Scott in 1740, includes a portion of Horace Waters' land, and others.

**Grandmother's Good Will,** granted to John Crampton, lies on the Little Seneca, and adjoins the farm of George W. Israel, south of Clarksburg.

**Cow Pasture,** surveyed for Henry Griffith, 10th February, 1761, for three thousand eight hundred and fifty-four and one-half acres, lies on both sides of Little Seneca Creek, near Clarksburg.

**Peach Tree Hill,** granted Richard Watts, September 13th, 1750, and contained seventy-five acres, and adjoins "Cow Pasture." A re-survey was granted for this tract to include vacancies, and called

**Errors Corrected,** for Nicholas Ridgely Warfield, May 23rd, 1792, containing two hundred and twenty-eight and three-fourths acres. The Little Seneca Creek passes through the tract, as also the Old Baltimore Road, from Barnesville to Neelsville. This is the home farm and residence of Gassaway W. Linthicum, and is under fine cultivation.

**Very Good,** granted to John Dickinson in 1755; and

**Bite the Biter,** granted to Samuel Saffell, in 1756, are both near the village of Damascus.

**Silent Valley,** granted to Ellsworth Beane in 1756, lies east of Damascus.

**Trouble Enough Indeed,** granted to Thomas Whitten, in 1761, contains two thousand four hundred and ninety-two acres, lies between Clarksburg and Damascus, and embraces the lands near King's Distillery.

By glancing at the map of the County, and starting from a point on the Patuxent, east of Richard H. Griffith's residence, and draw a line to William Griffith's residence on Hawlings'

River, thence to Brookeville, thence to Redland, thence to
Charles Saffell's residence, thence to F. A. Tschiffely's residence, thence to where the river road crosses Watts' Branch,
thence up the river road to the road from Poolesville to White's
Ferry, thence west to the Potomac River, a tolerably well defined
boundary line of the settlements made before 1730 will be had,
excepting a few mentioned settlements made on the head-waters
of the Great Seneca and the Dry Seneca. Beyond this boundary line but very few settlements were made previous to 1741.
Within these limits the settlement went on regularly as before,
but after 1741, the settlements again rapidly extended all over
the County, so that by 1775 very little vacant land remained.
After this period only here and. there a vacancy was discovered,
and then a re-survey on the adjacent tract would be made to
include the vacancy or vacancies.

From the earliest settlement to 1700, the grants were given
as lying in Charles County; from 1700 to 1745, they were given
as lying in Prince George's County; from 1745 to 1776, they
were given as lying in Frederick County; and since 1776, all
grants have been from Montgomery County.

# CHAPTER VIII.

*Frederick City. Georgetown, D. C. Tobacco. Rolling Roads. French War. Defeat of General Braddock. Massacre of the Settlers. The Revolution. Meeting at old Hungerford Tavern. Resolutions. Formation of Montgomery County, — Named after General Richard Montgomery. Rockville,—the County Seat. Districts of the County. Orphans' Court. Registers of Wills. Members of the State Convention.*

FREDERICK, now the second city of the State, was laid out 1745, and made the County town in 1748,—at which time Frederick County was formed, having been carved out of Prince George's.

GEORGETOWN was laid out in 1751 by an Act of the General Assembly, which set forth there was a convenient site for a town at the mouth of Rock Creek on the *Potowmack* River, adjacent to the Inspection House, called George Gordon's Rolling House, and that Captain Henry Wright Crabb, John Needham, John Clagett, James Perrie, Samuel Magruder the 3rd, Josias Beall, and David Lynn, should be commissioned for Frederick County, and authorized to purchase sixty acres of Messrs. George Gordon and George Beall, at the place aforesaid, to be erected into a town called *George Town.* For the advantage of the town and encouragement of the *back inhabitants*, the Commissioners were authorized to hold two Fairs annually, for three successive days, during which every one attending the same should be free from arrest, except for felony or breach of the peace. In 1783, a tract of land called the *Rock of Dumbarton*, belonging to Thomas Beall, was added to the town. In 1789, the town was incorporated, and Robert Peter was appointed Mayor, and John Mackall Garrett, Recorder. Brooke Beall, Bernard O'Neal, Thomas Beall of George, James McCubbin

Lingan, John Thirlkeld, and John Peter, Aldermen, so long as they shall well behave themselves therein.

Falling within the limits of the "ten miles square" that were ceded to the United States, by the States of Maryland and Virginia, in 1792, it has ever since formed a part of the District of Columbia.

The settlers multiplied and prospered, and the remunerative prices obtained for tobacco, which could be so successfully grown on their new lands, stimulated their enterprise. There was a great stir and much activity displayed when the tobacco was ready for market. The huge and stout hogsheads were fitted up with rough shafts, fastened to cleets, in which revolved the strong axle like pins inserted in either end. A single horse was attached, and the driver walking by the side, began to "roll" his tobacco to the market-town, generally Georgetown or Elk Ridge Landing. Some of these roads are still known as "Rolling Roads."

Their lives were spent in harmony and peace, until the breaking out of the French War, and the defeat of General Braddock in 1755, and the invasion of the western frontier of the province by the French and Indians from Fort Du Quesne. A period of terror and desolation ensued; the settlements were attacked and broken up; the outposts driven in; and some of the smaller posts captured and their garrisons massacred. More than twenty plantations were laid waste, and their occupants massacred or carried into captivity.

A force was organized from the lower district of Frederick County, (now Montgomery,) under Colonel Ridgely and Captain Alexander Beall, who went to the rescue and afforded protection to the settlers. General Braddock marched through this County on his ill-fated expedition, and encamped for one night within the present limits of Rockville. After the excitement attending the French and Indian War had subsided, nothing of military or political interest occurred, until the convulsions immediately preceding the Revolution.

When the news reached the people that the British had blockaded the port of Boston, a meeting was called at the famous old Hungerford Tavern, the proceedings of which were as follows:

## "FREDERICK COUNTY, MD., RESOLUTIONS."

"At a meeting of a respectable and numerous body of the freemen of the lower part of Frederick County, at Charles Hungerford's Tavern, on Saturday, the 11th day of June, 1774. Mr. Henry Griffith, Moderator.

"*1st. Resolved unanimously*, That it is the opinion of this meeting, that the town of Boston is now suffering in the common cause of America.

"*2nd. Resolved unanimously*, That every legal and constitutional measure ought to be used by all Americans for procuring a repeal of the Act of Parliament for blocking up the harbor of Boston.

"*3rd. Resolved unanimously*, That it is the opinion of this meeting, that the most effectual means for the securing of American freedom will be to break off all commerce with Great Britain and the West Indies, until the said Act be repealed, and the right of taxation given up on permanent principles.

"*4th. Resolved unanimously*, That Mr. Henry Griffith, Dr. Thomas Sprigg Wootton, Nathan Magruder, Evan Thomas, Richard Brooke, Richard Thomas, Zadok Magruder, Dr. William Baker, Thomas Cramphin, Jr., and Allen Bowie, be a Committee to attend the General Committee at Annapolis, and of Correspondence for the lower part of Frederick County, and that any six of them shall have power to receive and communicate intelligence to and from the neighboring Committees.

"*5th. Resolved unanimously*, That a copy of these our sentiments be immediately transmitted to Annapolis and inserted in the Maryland Gazette.

"ARCHIBALD ORME, *Clerk*."

Frederick County proper did not call a similar meeting until the 20th of June, nine days later.

The Committee which met at Annapolis appointed Matthew Tilghman, Thomas Johnson, Robert Goldsborough, William Paca, and Samuel Chase, members of the State Committee of Safety and Correspondence.

The territory now became too extensively peopled to remain under one municipal government, and, in 1776, was divided into three district municipalities, viz: Frederick County, constituting the central; Washington County, the upper; and Montgomery County, the lower division. Montgomery County was named after the gallant General Richard Montgomery, who fell on the Heights of Quebec in 1775, yielding up his life in the heroic attempt to rescue the Canadas from the dominion of Great Britain, and secure them to the then struggling cause of liberty in the American Colonies.

This was the first County that ignored the custom of naming towns and counties after princes, lords and dukes, and adopting in their stead illustrious republican names. As subdivisions went on, and new counties were formed, such pretentious names as My Lord Baltimore, Lord Frederick, Lord Arundel, and Prince George, gave way before advancing ideas, and names made memorable, both in the civil and military service, appeared, viz: Washington, Carroll, Howard, and Garrett—all distinguished by a long and honorable career as eminent citizens and public officers.

The first efforts towards the organization of Montgomery County was made by Dr. Thomas Sprigg Wootton, a member of the State Convention, who, on the 31st of August, 1776, presented to the President of the Convention, an Ordinance for the division of Frederick County into three distinct and separate counties,—which was read and ordered to lie on the table.

On the 6th of September following the Ordinance was again called up, and passed by a small majority. In relation to Montgomery County, it

*Resolved*, That after the first day of October next, such part of the said County of Frederick, as is contained within the bounds and limits following, to wit: Beginning at the east side of the mouth of Rock Creek on the Potomac River, and running thence with the said river to the mouth of the Monocacy, then with a straight line to Par's Spring, from thence with the line of the County to the beginning, shall be and is hereby erected into a new County called MONTGOMERY COUNTY.

In the succeeding year ROCKVILLE was selected as the County-seat. It was then but a small hamlet, with several small holdings, including Hungerford's Tavern, which is still standing and occupied by Mrs. Susan Russell, whose grandfather, Joseph Wilson, built and owned it, and the Anderson house, in which Miss Julia Anderson lives. The old court-house was built shortly afterwards, and the first Court held in 1779.

On the 3rd of August, 1784, William Prather Williams purchased the land surrounding the court-house, and immediately caused it to be laid off into streets and town lots by Col. Archibald Orme, County Surveyor, and named it Williamsburg.

At the November Session, 1801, of the General Assembly of the State, an Act was passed, which, after reciting that the titles to these lots were uncertain, because there was no record of the survey thereof made by Col. Orme, erected the place into a town called Rockville, and appointed Commissioners to re-survey it.

At the November Session, 1802, there was a supplemental Act passed, and, in 1803, the Commissioners caused the re-survey and a plan of the town to be made by William Smith, County Surveyor, which is recorded in Liber L., of the Land Records of the County.

It was at first contemplated to call the town Wattsville, but Watts' Branch being regarded as too insignificant a stream, it was finally concluded to honor its more assuming neighbor, Rock Creek, and hence the name, Rockville.

The old Hungerford, or Russell House, is not only the oldest building in the place, but also, from its associations, the object of greatest interest to the antiquary. Mrs. Richard Wootton, a sister-in-law of that Thomas Sprigg Wootton who moved the erection of the County, danced at a ball given in it one hundred and nine years ago.

The new County having been erected and furnished with a capital, it soon became necessary to lay it off into precincts; and, in 1798, an Act of Assembly was passed to divide it into five election districts, which was affirmed in 1799; and, in the same year, Daniel Reintzell, Hezekiah Veitch, Thomas Fletchall, John Adamson, and Thomas Davis, were appointed Commissioners, and marked out its five divisions, consisting of Rockville district, Medley's district, Berry's district, Cracklin district, and Clarksburg district.

In 1878, the County was re-districted and divided into eight election precincts, viz: First district, Cracklin; Second district, Clarksburg; Third district, Medley's; Fourth district, Rockville; Fifth district, Berry's; Sixth district, Darnestown; Seventh district, Bethesda; Eighth district, Mechanicsville.

The political and territorial organization of the County was completed, and the first Court held at the house of Leonard Davis, on the 20th of May, 1777,—the memorable old Hungerford Tavern, only Leonard Davis had succeeded Charles Hungerford as host. Present:—the Worshipful Charles Jones, Samuel W. Magruder, Elisha Williams, William Deakins, Richard Thompson, James Offutt, and Edward Burgess; Brook Beall, Clerk; Clement Beall, Sheriff.

The first Register of Wills was Samuel West, who served until the close of 1777, when he was succeeded by Richard Wootton.

Orphans' Courts and Registers of Wills were established in 1777. These Courts at first consisted of seven Justices of the Peace in the several counties, any three of whom constituted a quorum.

The present system, except that the Justices were appointive instead of elective, was established in 1790. The first Justices under the new system were Thomas Cramphin, Jr., Richard Wootton, and William Holmes. The names of the Justices who first served as Judges of the Orphans' Court, under the old system, have been lost, as no record of them can be found in the County.

The members from this County, to the State Convention of 1776, were Thomas Sprigg Wootton, Jonathan Wilson, William Bayly, Jr., and Elisha Williams.

## CHAPTER IX.

*A Period of One Hundred and Forty Years. The First Continental Congress. Maryland Convention. Enrollment and Organization of Companies. The First Blood shed in the Revolutionary War, 19th April, 1775. Captain Cresap's Company. Their Bravery in battle. Powder Mills. Cannon Manufactories. Contingent called from Montgomery County. The deeds of prowess in Virginia and the Carolinas. Revolutionary Officers from the County. The War of 1812. Distinguished Officers in the War of the Rebellion.*

THE First Continental Congress met at Philadelphia, on the 5th of September, 1774. It issued a Manifesto, setting forth the rights and grievances of the Colonies, and, on its adjournment, the Maryland Convention assembled and approved of the proceedings of the Congress. The power and dominion of the last Proprietary of Maryland closed with the organization of this Convention.

A period of one hundred and forty years had passed since two hundred pioneers, under Leonard Calvert, landed at Saint Mary's; their descendants had extended themselves throughout the length and breadth of its boundaries; covered the Eastern Shore with wealth and civilization,—crossed the Blue Ridge, filling its valleys with a bold and hardy population. Commerce was filling its bays and rivers with fleets; the forge and furnace were already at work, although burdened by the restrictive laws of England;—the germs of her future prosperity were budding forth and giving promise of the greatness which this day sees realized. Thus stood the people of Maryland in the crisis which was approaching; liberal in their sentiments, proud of their liberties, prepared to extend them, and ready to maintain them with their lives.

The Convention called upon the people of Maryland to bury all private animosities, all religious disputes, all memory of past persecution, and "in the name of God, their country and posterity, to unite in defence of the common rights and liberties." The Convention again assembled on the 8th of December, 1774, to make preparations for an armed resistance to the power of England. The old government still retained the form and machinery of power; the new, without these, possessed an irresistible authority throughout the colony. The source of its power was not its legal form, but public sentiment. Resting on this, it needed not penalties and judicial tribunals, for the dominion that has public sentiment for its throne is irresistible. Those who refused to submit to the decrees of the Convention were denounced by that body, and from that moment the offenders became the objects of scorn and contempt of their countrymen.

The Convention then ordered all males, from sixteen to fifty years of age, to be enrolled and organized into companies; to be armed, equipped and drilled, ready for instant service. These orders were immediately carried out; old and young enrolled with the greatest enthusiasm. Maryland was preparing herself for the struggle, in which she won so glorious a name.

On the 19th of April, 1775, the struggle culminated in open conflict, and the first blood shed in the Revolutionary War was at Lexington. After the battle of Bunker Hill there was no more hesitation; Congress determined, not only to defend the rights of the people, but to drive out the British troops. Thomas Johnson, of Maryland, had the honor of nominating General Washington as Commander-in-chief of the American forces.

The Convention again met on the 26th July, 1775, and ordered the formation of a regular force, to be composed of a battalion, of which Colonel Smallwood received the command, and seven independent companies, numbering in all 1444, besides two companies of artillery and one of marines.

By a resolution of Congress, two companies of riflemen were called for from Maryland. These companies were soon filled with the hardy pioneers of Montgomery and Frederick Counties. Captain Cresap's company numbered one hundred and thirty men, who were armed with tomahawks and rifles; were painted like Indians, and dressed in hunting shirts and moccas-

sins. These men were ordered to march to the camp around
Boston, being joined by like companies from Virginia and Pennsylvania. The arrival of these stalwart fellows, such as Washington had known in his early campaigns, many of them six
feet and upwards in height, and of vigorous frame—in their
fringed frocks and round hats, excited great wonder among the
rustic visitors of the camp. Their dash, their skill—"they
could hit a mark while advancing at quickstep, at the distance
of two hundred and fifty yards,"—their striking costume, caused
them to be looked upon with jealousy by the plainer troops
about them,—who seemed to think that all valor, as well as
virtue, was enclosed in the round jacket and trowsers of Mar-
blehead,—and it was well for the gaily clad sons of the South,
that their behaviour in battle was always equal to the expecta-
tion they excited. In the sharpest conflict of the war, it was
they "who stemmed the current of the bloody fight." The
officers of these were Michael Cresap, Thomas Warren, Joseph
Cresap, Jr., Richard Davis, Thomas Price, Otho H. Williams,
and John Ross Key. Many were too impatient to endure the
delay of organizing these troops, and hastened to join the camp
before Boston, at their own expense. Among these was James
Wilkinson, afterwards a Major-General in the United States'
service.

Great difficulty was experienced in obtaining supplies, the
arsenal at Annapolis was almost empty. To overcome these
difficulties, the Convention gave encouragement and gratuities
for the manufacture of saltpetre, materials for clothing and
munitions of war. Powder mills were erected, and Mr. Hughes,
of Montgomery County, agreed to furnish cannon for the province, and established a foundry on the Potomac River, at
Green Spring, one mile above Georgetown, where the first
cannon were made in this country,—a portion of the old stone
building still remains, while broken fragments of cannon are at
this time to be found in the stream of water that flows at the
base of the building.

The Convention having resolved to enroll forty companies of
minute men, required eight or one-fifth of the whole to be raised
in Frederick County, which then included what is now Montgomery and Washington Counties.

5

In raising the State contingent to reinforce the Federal armies in 1778, two years after the formation of Montgomery County, of the whole number, 2902 men required, Frederick's quota was 309, Montgomery's was 156, and Washington's 108 men, about the same proportion, one-fifth.

The two batallions required from Maryland for the relief of Boston were both selected from Montgomery and Frederick Counties, and from the number of officers from Montgomery who survived the Revolution and joined the Cincinnati Society at its close, it will be seen that a large portion not only of those troops, but of the entire Maryland line, were from this County. The names of the members of the Cincinnati Society were, C. Ricketts, Lieutenant; Lloyd Beall, Captain; Samuel B. Beall, Lieutenant; Henry Gaither, Captain; Richard Anderson, Captain; James McCubbin Lingan, Captain; Richard Chiderson, Captain; David Lynn, Captain. In addition to the members of that Society were Colonels Charles Greenbury Griffith and Richard Brooke; Captains Edward Burgess and Robert Briscoe; Lieutenants Greenbury Gaither, John Gaither, Elisha Beall, Elisha Williams, John Lynn and John Courts Jones; Ensigns Thomas Edmonson, John Griffith and William Lamar, and Quartermaster Richard Thompson, all from this County.

It was a dark hour that the Maryland line was destined to enter the field. On the 10th of July, 1776, six days after the passage of the Declaration of Independence, six companies under Colonel Smallwood, and three from Baltimore, embarked for the head of Elk River, whence they marched to New York, and were incorporated in Lord Stirling's Brigade. They were well appointed and organized, composed of young and spirited men, who had already acquired the skill and presence of well drilled soldiers. No unofficer-like appearance and deportment could be tolerated by the Marylanders, who at this time were distinguished by the most fashionable cut coats, the most stylish of cocked hats, and the *hottest blood* in the Union. On their arrival they immediately won the confidence of the Commander-in-Chief, and from the moment of their arrival, were thrown upon the advanced posts, and disposed as covering parties.

The four independent companies remaining in Maryland, as was also the flying camp, were ordered to join Col. Smallwood.

The achievements and deeds of valor performed by the officers and men in the desperate battles on Long Island, White Plains, Fort Washington, Trenton and Princeton, gave to the Old Maryland Line its synonym for heroic valor and devoted patriotism. During this campaign, a most dark and bloody one, but full of glory to the Maryland Line, the regiment was reduced to a mere handful of men under the command of a captain. The old line was almost annihilated.

It having been found necessary to establish an army in the South for the purpose of re-conquering South Carolina and Georgia from the British, and drive the invaders from North Carolina, the Maryland Line was detached from the main army, near New York in April, 1780, and marched through New Jersey, Pennsylvania, and embarked at the head of Elk River for Baltimore. The first and second brigades were immediately filled up, and passed through the State early in May, numbering about two thousand men, many of whom were from Montgomery and Frederick Counties. The most of that gallant and veteran army looked for the last time upon their beloved State; they offered up their lives in the defence of their brothers in the South. Their deeds of prowess, from the battle of Camden, where, under the command of Colonel Otho H. Williams, of Montgomery County, General Smallwood, and Colonel John Eager Howard, including the bloody struggles of Cowpens, Guilford Court House, Ninety-Six, Eutaw Springs, and the Surrender of Cornwallis at Yorktown, which took place on the 19th of October, 1781, nobly exemplifying the fact, that from the Heights of Brooklyn to the cotton fields of the Carolinas, the Maryland Line maintained their reputation for discipline and valor, worthy to be enrolled on monuments of marble and bronze. They were not mercenary soldiers, but farmers, merchants, and mechanics, who pledged their fortunes and lives to the cause of liberty.

The officers, elected by the Convention for this County, consisted of Colonels, John Murdock and Zadok Magruder; Lieutenant Colonels, Thomas Johns and Charles G. Griffith; First Majors, Richard and Francis Deakins; Second Majors, William Deakins and Richard Crabb; Quarter-Master, Samuel DuVall. These were the representative men of the day, and as sponsors of the cause of independence and freedom in its infancy, are worthy of perpetual remembrance.

Montgomery County furnished soldiers for the War of 1812, in which Major George Peters served with distinction. At the battle of Bladensburg, in 1814, the militia from this County and Prince George's, under the command of Commodore Barney, aided by a body of seamen and marines, maintained their ground until they were overpowered by numbers, and the Commodore taken prisouer. The enemy then proceeded to Washington, burned the Capitol, President's house and many other buildings. President Madison was compelled to take flight, and sought safety in Brookeville, in this County, from whence he issued his dispatches. In the late war between the sections, a large force entered the armies. Among the officers in the Confederate service, none were more distinguished for capacity, efficiency and valor, than the lamented Colonel Ridgely Brown, Colonel Elijah Veirs White, Colonel T. H. S. Boyd, Colonel Gus Dorsey and Colonel Benjamin S. White. In addition to these, there were Captains Thomas Griffith, Festus Griffith, George W. Chiswell and James Anderson, and Lieutenant Edward Chiswell, Surgeon Edward Wootten, and a host of other officers, non-commissioned officers and privates, all of revolutionary descent, and who, whether in a good or bad cause, illustrated the valor of the race and well maintained the reputation of the old Maryland Line.

So, from the first French and Indian War upon our borders, to the late sectional struggle, the people responded with alacrity to what they conceived to be the call of military duty. Their hearts ever glowing with the fire of patriotism.

## CHAPTER X.

*First Revolutionary Soldier. Montgomery's Revolutionary Roll. Pension Acts. Names of Pensioners. Meteoric Showers, as witnessed at the home of Charles Saffell, the Oldest Pensioner on the List. Scenes in Gaithersburg and Rockville.*

THE first Revolutionary soldier pensioned in Montgomery County was James Carrant. He was placed on the roll in compliance with the general Invalid Pension Law, approved June 7th, 1785, and died September 4th, 1822. Francis Hutchinson was also a pensioner, but not revolutionary. He belonged to the regular army of the United States. Samuel Harris was pensioned as a matross of the revolutionary artillery, and died on the 19th of September, 1826; and William A. Needham was also a revolutionary pensioner, placed on the roll in 1808. William O'Neal, was a private in the Maryland militia at some period not known, and placed on the pension roll, per Act April 30th, 1816, at the rate of $48 per annum; and Samuel B. White was a private in the revolutionary army, pensioned per Act June 7th, 1785, and died January 16th, 1832. James White was also a pensioner, per Act June 7th, 1785. He belonged to the revolutionary army, but the time of his death is not known. All the soldiers named above were invalid pensioners, pensioned on account of wounds and disability received in the service of the United States, *in the line of their duty*, and they honorably appear on old Montgomery's roll of honor, as good men, tried and true.

The following revolutionary soldiers, residing in Montgomery County, were pensioned by an Act of Congress, approved the 18th of March, 1818. In order to obtain the benefit of this Act, they were required to prove nine months service in the Continental army, and exhibit, under oath, a schedule showing that their property was worth no more than $500. Another Act was passed on the 1st of May, 1820, requiring the exhibition of another schedule, and, if in the meantime, their property had increased, so as to exceed $500 in value, they were dropped from the pension roll. These Acts of Congress were very distasteful to the old soldiers, for they looked upon them as offering a reward to soldiers for keeping themselves in poverty. The first name in the County placed on the pension roll, in compliance with the Act of 1818, was John Robbins, on the 6th of April, 1818, aged 72 years, at the rate of $96 per annum. He belonged to the "Old Maryland Line," so distinguished in all the battles in which it took a part. All the pensioners under this Act, if privates, received $96 per annum; if commissioned officers, they were allowed $240 per annum. The second name placed on the roll was that of Joseph Ray, aged 65 years, also of the Maryland Continental Line. Then followed the names of Thomas Penefill, aged 72 years, who died December 15th, 1832; James Ervin, aged 67, who died June 28th, 1827; George Field, aged 80, time of death unknown; Robert Hurdle, aged 75, time of death unknown; John Jordon, aged 77, time of death unknown; Henry Leeke, age not given, dropped from the roll per Act May 1st, 1820, time of death unknown. These were privates of the Maryland Line.

James Campbell, of Virginia Line, aged 71 years, private, died September 14th, 1827; Beltzor Lohr, Pennsylvania Line, aged 76, private, died February 27th, 1827; Thomas Lingan, Lieutenant, Maryland Line, aged 67, died May 28th, 1825; William Layman, Ensign, Maryland Line, aged 81, dropped from the roll per Act May 1st, 1820, restored March 22nd, 1826, time of death unknown. The two officers last named were pensioned at the rate of $240 per annum.

The following named soldiers of the revolutionary war, residing in the County, were pensioned per Act of Congress, approved June 7th, 1832. The minimum rate of pension allowed a private under this Act, was $20 per annum for six months service in any department of the revolutionary army, and increased, *pro rata*, according to the time of service, so as not to exceed the rate of $80 per annum, the maximum, for two years service. No grade of officer was allowed more than $600 per annum, for two years service. Periods of service for less than two years, were rated according to rank and time of service. Every soldier was entitled to pension under this Act, without regard to the value of his property, and many who lost their pensions on the passage of the Act of May 1st, 1820, were restored by the Act of 1832. All pensions under this Act were made to commence on the 4th of March, 1831. Those pensioned were as follows:

| | | | | | |
|---|---|---|---|---|---|
| Geo. Beckwith, Sergeant, | $32.50 | per ann., | Maryland Line, | age | 74. |
| Richard Barrett, " | 36.15 | " | " | " " | 79. |
| Giles Easton, Private, | 30.00 | " | " | " " | 73. |
| Caleb Galworth, " | 80.00 | " | " | " " | 77. |
| Chas. Morris, Corporal, | 79.66 | " | New York | " " | — |
| Chas. Saffell, Musician, | 88.00 | " | Maryland | " " | 84. |
| Joseph Warfield, Lieutenant, | 85.97 | " | " | " " | 76. |
| Saml. Griffith, Captain, | 414.00 | " | " | " " | — |
| James Fling, Private, | 80.00 | " | Virginia | " " | 73. |

Charles Saffell, the oldest man on the list, died in 1837.

The following thrilling account of a visit to the home of this old veteran, on the occasion of the great Meteoric Showers on the night of the 12th of November, 1833, four years previous to his death, will be interesting.

"Five miles beyond the mill, (Clopper's on the great Seneca,) at early candle-light, I reined up at the farm of Charles Saffell, an old soldier, then 84 years of age, who had been a musician in the Revolutionary Army. The old gentleman had a drum, fife and fiddle, an old English musket, which he captured at the battle of Brandywine, and many other relics from the 'days that tried men's souls.' He was spending the calm evening of his long life in singing our long catalogue of heroes, yet unsung; and from his sweet flute, fife and violin I ardently drank in the inspiring melodies of the revolution. At the hour of ten o'clock I took a candle and a row of paper matches, about the length and appearance of a row of pins, and retired to bed in an upper room. The matches were made by cutting out a piece of paper about three inches long, and one wide, and making a dozen clips with a pair of scissors, into one of the longer edges of the paper so prepared, as to extend about three-quarters of the distance across its width. This clipped edge was dipped into the combustible mixture, and when dry, all that was necessary to produce a flame, was to tear off one of these clippings and draw its dipped ends gently along between the tip of the forefinger and the wall of your room, or over the surface of any other rough substance. I struck the match, the first kind known in trade, and with a cheerful and glad heart lit the candle. I was under the cover and yielded to tired nature's sweet restorer, but soon encountered very singular and inexplicable experience, which I will mention, for I am writing facts, of which I ought not to be ashamed. The air being keen and frosty, three counterpanes were on the bed, and I slid under them and made a survey of the surroundings in the dark room before trying my hand at sleep. On entering the room I discovered a wooden bolt on the door and made it fast against intrusion; saw several chairs, other articles of furniture, and two windows only, over which curtains were hanging, one of them being at the back of the bed, within reach of the occupant. Trying my hand at sleep, I met with half success, but just at this stage of proceeding, imagine my surprise when, by some unseen force, the three counterpanes were drawn violently from the bed to the floor! After recovering from my surprise and fright, I visited the ruins on the floor, recaptured the counterpanes, and courted sleep once more. After a time, I fell into a troubled sleep, and down went the counterpanes again with greater violence than at first. I sprang down after them, found the matches, lit the candle, and searched for the intruder, but no such party could be found, neither in nor under the bed, nor elsewhere in the room.

"I made up the bed again, got in, tried to sleep, but the fates had decreed that I should not, for sleep had departed to climes to me unknown. After a long trial, I know not how long, I nervously fell into its arms again, but was suddenly roused by a terrific stream of unearthly light, flashing through the window, curtain and all, and blazing over the room from floor to ceiling! Suddenly drawing the curtain aside, I beheld a great ball of fire, as large as the sun and moon, appear, rushing from the direction of the zenith, and describing a circular or parabolic curve towards the far distant south-western horizon! Hearing at the same time a great uproar among the servants down in the yard, I sprang from the bed to the next window, and looked out upon the great Meteoric shower of the 12th and 13th of November, 1833. Rushing down into the yard, I saw a squad of frightened servants, so terrified indeed that they knew nothing save that the world was coming to an end. The old soldier appeared at the door, asked me to come into his room, and said it was nothing—he had seen the like before. The shower continued till overpowered by daylight, the stars rushing down through space like snow-flakes, yet vastly more luminous. Fearful balls of fire shot madly towards the earth, like the pyrotechnic rocket shoots upward, consuming their substance in flight, or losing it by friction against the walls of air. Most of the meteors were as large and brilliant as the stars themselves; and it required no vivid imagination to suppose that these celestial bodies were then rushing down to earth; for the heavens blazed with an incessant discharge of fiery globes that burst in countless numbers from the cloudless sky.

"Leaving the old soldier's house, I hurried on to Rockville, through Gaithersburg, looking all along the road for traces of the great phenomenon; some natural record or engraving of its occurrence; but could discover none, save in the eternal flint of words and memory. All whom I talked with on the way took a religious view of the case, none venturing an astronomical or meteorological solution of the great problem so suddenly sprung upon them. It was therefore generally believed that the time had come when 'the stars of heaven shall fall,' and when 'the powers of the heaven shall be shaken,' for the confusion was so great that not one could call to mind the fact that the great Egyptian, Grecian, Roman and Jewish stars of empire and powers of heaven, referred to by the great Teacher and Prophet, had already fallen along the Mediterranean shores, to make way for other great stars of empire, climbing the canopy of nations, and holding their way westward.

"At Gaithersburg, and on the road from that village to Rockville, I met great numbers of people hurrying to and fro, that their knowledge might be increased. The theory that all the stars *were down* and that not a luminary would blaze and twinkle in the heavens during the coming night, was generally supported by those who took a Biblical view of the matter on their 'own hook;' but such as had the least claim to common sense, knew better, and sought an explanation somewhere outside of the lids of the Bible.

"About 9 o'clock on the morning of the 13th, I reined up before the old hotel in Rockville, and soon entered the bar-room, but I shall break down in the attempt to describe appearances in that room, in front of the door, on the porch, in the street, and wagon-yard,—not that I did not see and remember well enough to do so—but that description was so beggared that no pen was, nor is, adequate to the task.—I saw lawyers, physicians, ministers, farmers, wagoners, sportsmen in the chase, and at the card-table—all repenting of their sins; confessing to one another; taking and denying positions, and covering up tracks. Certain of them confessed that when they first saw the raging meteoric shower cast its globes of fire to the ground, and against the outside walls and the windows of their room, they rushed from the card-table, cast their pack into the fire, and kneeled in prayer before a long neglected throne of mercy. They prayed ardently, it is said, until the shower was overpowered by daylight, and just as I entered the bar-room, I saw some of the accused coming down stairs with elongated faces unwashed, uncombed hair, unbrushed clothing, unblacked boots, and caved-in beavers! One excited orator stood forth in the bar-room, and declared that every man, who believed the big stars had fallen, was a fool; for he had watched them during the whole time of the shower, and not one of them had forsaken its post in the heavens. 'When night comes,' said he, 'you may miss some of the little stars, but my word for it, the big ones will be there.' Countrymen on their way to market declared that they saw great stars fall, explode and bury their fragments in the earth.

"I soon left for Georgetown to gain experience there; and here, in conclusion, I remark, that persons grown up since the year 1833, can never obtain an idea of the great meteoric shower worthy of the name of an idea, for it must be seen only to be realized, and that by large and cultivated capacities."

# CHAPTER XI.

*First Member of Congress from this County. Whiskey Insurrection in Pennsylvania. Names of Montgomerians who served in the Federal Congress. Hon. Montgomery Blair as Cabinet Minister. Members of Reform State Conventions, 1850–51, 1864, 1867. First County Surveyor. First Schools. An Act for Purchasing School Property. Academies, Colleges, &c., and their Students. First Church in the County, Parson Williamson, Rector.*

THE first Member of Congress from this County was General JEREMIAH CRABB, a member of one of the first Congresses. At the close of the Revolutionary war, he received a commission as General from General George Washington, and was employed against the whiskey insurrectionists in Pennsylvania. This was occasioned by the first attempt at obtaining a revenue from internal taxes, by an Act, passed in 1791, imposing duties on domestic distilled spirits. This Act had from the first been very unpopular in many parts of the country. During this year the attempts to enforce the Act led to open defiance of the laws in the western counties of Pennsylvania. After two ineffectual proclamations by the President, he was compelled to call into action a large military force, in order to quell the insurgents.

The names of the different gentlemen who have at various periods since served in the Federal Congress, from this County, are, PATRICK MAGRUDER, THOMAS PLATER, PHILIP BARTON KEY, ALEXANDER CONTEE HANSON, at one time Chancellor of the State, GEORGE PETER, GEORGE C. WASHINGTON, and RICHARD J. BOWIE, who has also held the position of Chief Judge of the Court of Appeals of Maryland, and is now one of the Associate Justices of that Court, and Chief Judge of the Sixth Judicial Circuit of this State. The County has also furnished one Cabinet Minister to the General Government—Hon. MONTGOMERY BLAIR; and two Presidents of the Maryland Senate—BENJAMIN S. FORREST and WILLIAM LINGAN GAITHER.

The members from this County of the Reform State Convention of 1850 and 1851, were Dr. WASHINGTON WATERS, JAMES W. ANDERSON, JOHN BREWER, ALLEN BOWIE DAVIS, and JOHN MORTIMER KILGOUR. Of the State Convention of 1864, Dr. EDMOND P. DUVALL, THOMAS LANSDALE and GEORGE PETER; and of the Convention ot 1867, Dr. NICHOLAS BREWER, Dr. WASHINGTON DUVALL, SAMUEL RIGGS of R. and GREENBURY M. WATKINS.

THOMAS DAVIS was Surveyor of the County in 1790, and besides being a good practical surveyor, was frequently elected to represent his native County in the Legislature, the Electoral College for electing the State Senators, under the old Constitution, and as a member of the Governor's Council. He served as a Justice of the Peace, a member of the Board of Tax Commissioners, Judge of the Levy and Orphans' Courts, and also was one of the Associate Judges of the County Court, before the change of the system requiring all three of the Judges to be taken from the legal profession. Besides these public duties, he was frequently called upon to draw deeds, wills and contracts, and to act as umpire or arbitrator in settling disputes between neighbors and other citizens of the County. He was also one of the founders and leading trustees of the Brookville Academy, and of St. Bartholomew's Protestant Episcopal Church, in whose Vestry and Communion he died in 1833, in the sixty-fifth year of his age, deeply lamented and mourned by a wide circle of friends and relatives,—a life worthy of record and imitation.

An Act for the encouragement of learning and erecting schools in the several Counties of the State, passed in 1723, enacted that one school should be established in each County, with seven visitors appointed for each, with power to hold lands to the value of one hundred pounds sterling per annum, and were required to purchase one hundred acres of land for the use of the school, and erect necessary buildings for master and school, and certain moneys were appropriated, and directed to be equally divided between the Counties.

The masters were required to teach as many *poor children as the Visitors should determine.* Under this law, County Schools were erected in all the older and more populous Counties.   In further pursuance of this policy, the Assembly of 1763, chapter 32, declaring it was reasonable that education should be extended equally to the several parts of the Province, and that there should be a Public School erected in Frederick County, as well as in other Counties.   In order to the erecting and building a house and other conveniences for a County School, enacted there should be one acre purchased in Frederick Town, in Frederick County; that Col. Thomas Cresap, Mr. Thos. Beatty, Mr. Nathan Magruder, Capt. Joseph Chapline, Mr. John Darnall, Col. Samuel Beall and the Rev. Mr. Thomas Bacon, be Visitors of the School, and authorized to purchase the lot.   It was further enacted that an equal dividend of the duties, taxes, &c., collected for the use of the County Schools, shall be paid to said Visitors, and applied to the purchase of said lots and buildings.

The Public School System, under the control of the Church of England, although tainted with the intolerance of the period, displays a commendable solicitude for the cultivation of the minds and morals of the youth of the Colony.   In the absence of Collegiate Institutions, Private Schools conducted by learned men, ecclesiastical and lay, of all creeds, laid the foundation of scholastic knowledge.   The more affluent youth were educated abroad; but the log school house, and the winter fireside, developed the seeds of science in many minds, and produced a race of men of extraordinary mental endowments and capacity for public affairs.

The first School of any reputation in the County, was a Seminary for young men, established towards the close of the Revolutionary War, by Mr. JAMES HUNT, a Presbyterian Clergyman from Philadelphia, on his farm called "TUSCULUM," now memorable as the Alma Mater of William Wirt.   It was here he was prepared, as far as scholastic training could prepare him, for that brilliant career which has made his name one of the most illustrious in American annals.

The next Classical Institution established in the County, was the ROCKVILLE ACADEMY, chartered in 1809, and the BROOKEVILLE ACADEMY next in 1814.   Both of these Institutions are handsomely endowed by the State, and have been in successful operation ever since their foundation, and have exerted a refining and elevating influence, not only on the youth of the County, but extending throughout the different sections of the country. Many private institutions of learning, of efficiency and reputation, have since been established at Rockville, Brookeville, Sandy Spring, Darnestown and Poolesville, while the Public School System is the best that could be devised. Involuntary ignorance is no longer possible, and ignorance of every kind is being rapidly eradicated.

A description of one of the early schools will be interesting, describing the scenes and incidents connected with education fifty years ago, at the BARNESVILLE ACADEMY, near the Village of Barnesville in this County. It was called in those days Hays' School House, and consisted of a room sixty feet long by thirty feet wide, built to accommodate about one hundred scholars; old style desks, carefully made with drawers for keeping the books in safe condition, were arranged around the walls, and along the middle of the floor. Two ten plate stoves, made for burning wood, half the cord stick in length, warmed the hall; shelves extended all around the upper part of the walls near the ceiling, for the storage of *grub* baskets; and nails were driven in the walls, close under these shelves, for the hanging up of cloaks, hats, bonnets and shawls. The principal's desk was placed at the south end of the hall. On it sat the bell, the much dreaded bell in "play time," whose sound must not be disregarded. Before it, reposed the *rattan*, a foreigner by growth, yet it frequently made itself too familiar with the school boys, for the comfort of the latter. Contrary to the general laws of war, it would attack them in the rear, and make retreat impossible.

The halcyon days of the academy were from 1830 to 1836; Thomas Carr Lannan, a graduate of Belfast College, Ireland, was the principal; and, for a time, Mr. Rogers and Mr. McGary, two young candidates for holy orders in the Catholic Church, his assistants.

Beginning with the young ladies, who graded high in Mr. Lannan's classes, comes Miss Henrietta Herwood, a beautiful and queenly young lady, sixteen or seventeen years of age, who came four miles to school, riding on the same horse behind her elder brother. She was an orphan and resided with the family of Richard A. Harding near the mouth of Monocacy;

Miss Mary Plummer, a mild and gifted young lady of sixteen, beautiful of face and form, with energies sufficient to induce her to scorn the foot of any class; Miss Caroline Murphy, the accomplished belle of the Sugar Loaf, so charming as to be able to break multitudes of strong hearts without her knowledge or consent. She rendered "Old Zip Coon" so sweetly on the piano, that, on oft-repeated occasions, the light fantastic toe of her admirers would be set in motion keeping time with the melody. Miss Martha Hayes, a very neat and handsome figure, deep blue eyes, and intellectual forehead and face; she wa gifted in conversation, and general favorite in the school. Miss Mary Nicholls a beautiful, intellectual, and winning young lady, bound to gravitate to the head of her class; Miss Frances Trail, who fell behind none of the above mentioned in accomplishments, and Miss Jane, her sister, a handsome blue-eyed girl, a sharp scholar, and general favorite; Miss Sarah Ellen Hays, a rare beauty, sweet singer, and an accomplished performer on the piano; Miss Ellen Jones, sixteen years old, beautiful and winning and a great favorite, highly esteemed by all her classmates; Miss Mary Pearre, sister of Judge Pearre of Allegany County, not less beautiful than her classmates, yet more affectionate than many—her face just as intellectual as fair, was always seen at the head of her class, or thereabouts; Miss Catharine Pearre, her sister—the words spoken of Mary are admirably adapted to her also; Miss Henrietta Wilcoxen, was the queen among the beauties of the County.

These young ladies bore the old names of the County which carried a prestige, socially, of dominant influence. They silently told the story of their well-bred existence to every one who saw them; and appeared to be, as they really were, the daughters of unostentatious gentlemen of the old school, who planted and built for themselves and their posterity.

The young gentlemen who attended the academy at this time were Edward Hays, Mortimore Trail, Oscar Trail, Thomas Nichols, Richard Belt, Thomas Harwood, John Sellman, Gassaway Grimes, Howard Sellman, Thomas Johnson, James Pearre, Thomas Austin, Stephen Jay, Pickering White, George Pearre, David Hershey, John Hershey, Lemuel Beall, Avery Bell, William Sellman, Richard Thompson, John Reid, Robert Sellman, William Saffell, Hamilton Anderson, King Jay, Reuben Carley, Philemon Plummer.

Gassaway Grimes, Richard Thompson and John Reid belonged to the higher Latin and Greek classes. They entered upon the study of medicine, graduated, and became very respectable in the profession.

Dr. THOMSON now lives in Clarksburg and has an extensive practice, surrounded by his children and grand-children; he bids fair to live long in the enjoyment of his pleasant surroundings. Dr. REID lives in Washington County; Dr. GRIMES died in early life, not long after he commenced practice.

Oscar Trail, Edward Hays, Richard Belt and Thomas Johnson belonged to the same class, and stood foremost in the academical course.

Mr. TRAIL commenced the mercantile business in Baltimore, where he became a highly respected and successfnl merchant, but, to the great regret of all his friends and classmates, died early in life, leaving a young family. Messrs. Hays, Belt and Johnson took up some learned profession.

GEORGE PEARRE studied law in Frederick, became learned in the profession, and removed to Cumberland, where he became a Judge of Allegany County, whose distinguished abilities on the Bench fully declare his worth.

WILLIAM and ROBERT SELLMAN were respectable and earnest scholars, bent on "a business education," which this school well afforded. They made successful business men, highly respected in the community; John is now residing in Baltimore in very easy circumstances, and has recently filled a seat in the City Council with much ability and favor. Robert is also in Baltimore, where he has, for a great number of years, held and is still holding, to the entire satisfaction of the mercantile community, the office of Inspector of Flour. William now resides in our County, and has recently represented it in the Senate of Maryland, in a manner very satisfactory to his constituents.

JOHN HERSHEY, a noble young man, went into the ministry, after winning many prizes in the Latin and Greek classes, and became a useful and prominent Minister of the Gospel.

At this school, the foundations for a thorough business education were well and truly laid down under the personal superintendence of the principal, and a training for the higher collegiate course was performed by him in a scholarly manner. All the Latin historians, poets, and orators occurring in the course between Jacob's Latin Reader, and the polished sentences of Tacitus were well read and understood, and a similar Greek course kept equal pace with the Latin. A "business education," as understood at the Barnesville Academy, consisted in reading through the "English Reader," committing to memory a definition of all the words in Walker's Small Dictionary, ciphering as far as the "Single Rule of Three" in Arithmetic, with Grammar from Murray or Kirkham, sufficient to qualify the student to write an essay or letter over a half sheet of the large foolscap paper used in that day. To this was added Single Entry Book-Keeping, done on unruled paper, stitched together for the purpose with needle and thread; but more frequently with awl and "wax end," obtained from shoe shops in the village. A balance sheet was struck at the end of six months, the course was finished, the student then graduated with "a business education" and retired from the school. This is what was generally understood as a business education fifty years ago.

Graduating with a business education, with brains sharpened for the contest, the student, instead of retiring to the pursuits of life, would often enter the higher classes, springing as a lion into the arena, then woe to the poor stragglers in the rear, for somebody must "step down and out," or make rapid strides towards the front.

After a course of gentle hazing, the new student was fully admitted into the society of the school. This was done by enticing the freshman into some amusing scrape with the principal, by ducking him in the snow in the winter; or he was by strategy on the part of the old regulars, repeatedly brought to "the knucks," at the game of marbles played in holes, until his hands were severely bruised. Mr. Lannan always made it a point to ascertain from the new scholar what business he wished to follow when grown up to manhood, and trained him accordingly, directing special and constant attention to the development of all his capacities in that direction.

Public examinations were periodically held at the Academy. For a month or more previous they were drilled for the great

6

competitive struggle, in hard questions calculated to span over every branch of study.

There was little or no literature in the early days of the County.

But the public archives, the proceedings, reports, resolutions, and letters of public men, embodied in the Journals of the Convention; the legislation of the State immediately succeeding its organization as an independent sovereign power; the judicial opinions and the brilliant career of members of the bar educated before and after, Martin, Pinkney, Wirt, Taney, Johnson, and men of that stamp, attest that the fountains from which they drank were both pure and invigorating.

The first church in the County was the Rock Creek Church, in the Parish of Prince George, which extended over a portion of Prince George's County, and what is now the District of Columbia, and the whole of Montgomery and Frederick Counties, but now only embraces a small territory around Rockville. Parson Williamson was the Rector in charge at the breaking out of the Revolutionary War, and built the fine old mansion of Hayes, formerly the seat of the Dunlaps, and now the property of William Laird, Esq. He was supported by the compulsory tithe system.

# CHAPTER XII.

*First Public Roads. Rolling Tobacco to Market. Union Turnpike. Washington, Colesville and Ashton. Columbia. The Old Baltimore. River Road. Old Annapolis. Conduit. Old Potomac Company. Subscriptions to said Company. Chesapeake and Ohio Canal. Coal Elevators in Georgetown. First Railroad in the Country. Baltimore and Ohio Railroad. Metropolitan Branch.*

THE first public roads mentioned in the County, are the roads from Georgetown to Frederick, and from Georgetown to Watts' Branch, provided for in the loan granted to the several Counties for road purposes, by the Act of Assembly, 1774. The next mention is of the road from Frederick to Georgetown, the road from Georgetown to the mouth of the Monocacy, and from the mouth of Monocacy to Montgomery Court House, (in the Act of Assembly, 1790, to straighten and amend the public roads in the several Counties.) The planters at that early period did not use wheeled vehicles, but attached a sapling to each end of a tobacco hogshead, and thus formed a pair of shafts, by which they hauled the hogsheads for shipment to Europe, to Bladensburg, Georgetown, Elk Ridge, and Baltimore, and brought back their supplies of groceries and other necessaries on the backs of horses. They even brought their annual supply of herring and shad in this manner. Their clothing and bed linen were chiefly woven from home-grown flax and wool. Their personal travel was done exclusively on horseback.

Roads after this period rapidly multiplied. The turnpike from Rockville to Georgetown, the first paved road in the County, was originally chartered in 1806; but was actually constructed under an amendatory Act, containing the chief provisions of its present charter, passed in 1817.

The Union Turnpike Road, leading from Washington to Brookeville, was chartered in 1849. It has recently built several branch roads.

The Washington, Colesville and Ashton Turnpike road, chartered in 1870.

The Columbia road runs from Washington to Westminster, passing through Brookeville.

The Old Baltimore road runs through the County, commencing on the Monocacy near its mouth.

The River road runs along the Potomac from Georgetown to White's Ferry.

The old Annapolis road runs from the Brookeville Turnpike, near Mitchell's Cross Roads to Annapolis.

The Conduit road from Georgetown to the Great Falls on the Potomac River, was completed in 1875. It follows the line of the Washington Aqueduct, and crosses Cabin John Branch on a bridge of a single arch, the longest span in the world. This Aqueduct is also a Montgomery County work, having its source and almost its entire line within the limits of the County, and its permissive right from the State of Maryland.

The initial movement towards internal improvement in North America, was inaugurated in this County, in 1774, two years before the Declaration of Independence, and ten years before the organization of the old Potomac Company. George Washington and Charles Carroll, of Carrollton, were conspicuous as promoters of the movement. The following is a copy of an old subscription paper, showing the names of the subscribers and the amounts.

" WE, the subscribers, have considered JOHN BALLENDINE'S plan and proposals for clearing *Potowmack River*, and do approve of it; and to enable him to set about that useful and necessary undertaking, do hereby agree and promise severally, to contribute such assistance, or pay such sums as we respectively subscribe, to the TRUSTEES named in the said plan and proposals, or to their order at such times and places, and in such proportions as shall be required by them, for the purpose of clearing the said RIVER. Witness our hands this TENTH DAY OF OCTOBER, ONE THOUSAND SEVEN HUNDRED AND SEVENTY-FOUR.

"N. B.—As nothing effectual can probably be done for less than about thirty thousand pounds, this subscription is not to be binding unless to the value of thirty thousand pounds, Pennsylvania Currency, should be subscribed.

"GEORGE WASHINGTON, five hundred pounds Virginia Currency;

"Ralph Wormely, " " " " "

"Th. Johnson, Jr., for self and Mr. L. Jacques, £500 Penn'a Cur'y.

"Dan of St. Thos. Jenifer, three hundred pounds, Dol'rs at 7s. 6d.

"Geo. Plaix, three hundred pounds, Currency.

"T. Ridout, two hundred pounds, Currency.

"Daniel Dulany's son Walter, £200, Currency.

"David Ross, for the Fredericksburg Co's, 500 pounds Pen'a Cur'y.

"David Ross, for himself, 300 pounds Pennsylvania Currency.

"Dan'l and Sam'l Hughes, five hundred pounds Penn. Currency.

"Benj. Dulany, five hundred pounds Pennsylvania Money.

"Thos. Ringgold, one thousand pounds, Pennsylvania Currency.

"W. Ellzey, one hundred pounds.

"Jonas Clapham, one hundred pounds, Virginia Currency.

"William Deakins, Jr., one hundered pounds—dollars, at 7s. 6d.

"Joseph Chapline, fifty pounds common current money.

"Tho. Richardson, fifty pounds, Pennsylvania Currency.

"Thomas Johns, fifty pounds, common Currency.

"Adam Stephen, two hundred pounds, Pennsylvania Currency.

"Robt. and Tho. Rutherford, one hundred pounds, Penn'a Cur'y.

"Francis Deakins, one hundred pounds, Com'n Cur'y of Maryland.

"CHARLES CARROLL, of Carrollton, £1000, Cur'cy, Dol. at 7s. 6d.

"By Act of Assembly in 1784, the State of Virginia gave to 'George Washington, Esq.,' fifty thousand shares, capital stock of the Potomac Company, and one hundred thousand shares of the James River Company's stock to testify their sense of 'his unexampled merits towards his country.' For this Washington returned his thanks in the most profound and grateful manner, but respectfully declined the gift; and in doing so, he uses these memorable words, which ought to be printed in gold over the door of every man who accepts high public trust,—'When I was called to the station with which I was honored during the late conflict for our liberties, I thought it to be my duty to join to a firm resolution to shut my hands against every pecuniary recompence; to this resolution I have invariably adhered; from this resolution (if I had the inclination) I do not consider myself at liberty to depart.'"

The old Potomac Company was chartered in 1784, and General Washington was its first President, and assisted in person in the survey of the river. The object of the Company, was to render the upper Potomac River navigable by the means of locks, dams and short canals.

The work was so far proceeded with as to afford a precarious navigation at high water for batteaux or flat bottomed boats, from Cumberland to Georgetown. But the route was exceedingly dangerous, and a great number of boats were wrecked every spring. The people of Cooney, a settlement on the Virginia shore of the Potomac, at and around its Little Falls, obtained from the wrecks a bountiful supply of flour, meat and groceries, and with the fish taken from the river, furnished them with their principal means of support.

The Chesapeake and Ohio Canal, which succeeded the old Potomac Canal, was first projected in 1823 by the States of Maryland, Virginia and Pennsylvania, and the National Government. It was chartered by the State of Virginia in 1824; but its organization was not completed until 1828. It is one of the greatest works of internal improvement in the country and of inestimable value to the people, extending as it does, along the entire Western border, and offering cheap transportation to some of the richest sections of the County.

An evidence of the magnitude of the business transmitted over the Canal in the one article of coal alone, can be formed from the number of boats unloaded at the elevators in Georgetown every year. Last year six thousand boats unloaded at these elevators, averaging one hundred and twelve tons each, making the total number of tons received, six hundred and seventy-two thousand. Some years past it has amounted to over one million tons. The facilities for unloading are so perfect, that from fifty to sixty boats can be unloaded per day. The freight from Cumberland is about eighty-five cents per ton, while the toll amounts to forty cents per ton. The Collector's office for the Company is at Georgetown, and William E. Porter is superintendent of the Canal Company. Mr. Porter is from Cecil County, and was appointed superintendent in 1878. Previous to this, he was with the Baltimore and Ohio Railroad Company for twenty-seven years, twenty years as assistant master and seven years as supervisor of the road. During the war he had general charge of repairing and constructing bridges west of Harper's Ferry. Previous to the battle of Winchester, General Shields ordered him to construct a suspension bridge across Back Creek, for the passage of his army. He accomplished the work in three hours, over which General Shields and his army of sixteen thousand men crossed in safety. Mr. Porter received the acknowledgments of the General after the battle.

The Collector is William Snowden, from Anne Arundel County, and has a thorough acquaintance with the duties of the office. Mr. F. M. Griffith, who has been connected with the Canal since 1870, is Assistant Collector, and is from Beallsville, Montgomery County.—Mr. James S. Kemp, of Clarksburg, Montgomery County, is Harbor Master, and is assisted by Mr. Frank Fisher, from near Darnestown, of this County.

In 1830, the Canal Company constructed a railroad four or five miles in length, to facilitate the transportation of stone from the great "White Quarry," at the foot of Sugar Loaf Mountain, for the building of an Aqueduct over the river Monocacy at its junction with the Potomac.

Excavations for the Baltimore and Ohio Railroad may have commenced before the excavations for this little mountain road, yet it is quite certain that here the first rails were laid, and here the first railroad in Maryland, and perhaps the first in the United States, was put in full operation. The Canal Company, in preparing to construct the great Aqueduct at the mouth of Monocacy, first thought of the transportation of ponderous hewn stone from the foot of the Sugar Loaf, by

routes over which wagons could not possibly pass, and proceeded to construct the first, and now almost forgotten railroad.
As short as it was, and diminutive as it appeared before other
great lines of road, which soon followed on its construction, it
should be described in the history of the County. Iron rails
were not used, the wooden ones, or "string pieces," as they
were called, consisted of nothing more than trunks of trees,
generally oak, cut from twelve to sixteen feet long, so as to
allow the diameter at the smaller end to be not less than eight
or ten inches. Along the whole length of these string pieces a
groove or triangular trough was cut with an adze from the cir-
cumference to the centre, taking out a fourth part of the wood,
which left two flat surfaces, forming a right angle at the heart
or centre of the log. The trackway was graded and the log, or
string piece, put down with one of its flat surfaces parallel with
the surface of the ground, and the other perpendicular to it.
The perimeter of the car-wheel ran on the flat surface of the
groove or trough, and the outside or outward edge of the perimeter moved along the perpendicular surfaces of the string
piece on each side of the track, holding the car firmly in its
place, and preventing it from running off to the ground. The
track was firmly ballasted on the inner and outer side with *blast
rock.* This was generally called, simply, *blarst* by the Irish
laborers, because it consisted of small pieces of rock thrown off
by blasting. A smooth path was made between the string
pieces to accommodate two horses abreast. No cross ties were
used; the weight of the string pieces and the stone ballast was
sufficient to bind the track together. When one flat surface of
the rail or string piece was worn and split by the pressure of
the wheel, the other was turned down by turning the rails "end
for end," or from "side to side," of the track, and thus the road
was repaired, until it became necessary to put in new string
pieces. The road was built up hill and down, through a rough
and mountainous country, for the greater part of the way—
very little grading being done. The cars consisted of a plain
wooden platform only, supported by iron wheels and axles.
One wheel, or more, on each car, had cogs on the inside of the
perimeter, into which an iron lever could play, so as to lock a
wheel or two in going down hill. The lever was held in the
hand of the driver of the horses; and when the wheel or wheels

were locked, the car, with its great load of hewn rock, would, to the relief of the horses, slide down the hill like a locked wagon on an earthen road. Snow was removed from the track by Irish laborers with shovels. A car containing tools and provisions, with "gigger" cups and big jugs, was dispatched from each terminus of the road to clean off snow, and when the two parties met on the road double giggers were dealt out by the "grog boss," and great hilarity pleasantly followed, unless the laborers happened to be hostile, and then an attempt might be made to repeat the battle of the Boyne. The road was kept in active operation until the Aqueduct was finished, and then abandoned to decay. Most of the string pieces, however, were soon seized by the mountaineers for firewood, and the ballast hauled off to build and repair stone fences.

The Baltimore and Ohio Railroad, the pioneer of all the great railroad systems of the world, was chartered in 1827. This is not strictly a Montgomery work, and nowhere touches the County, yet as it, together with its Washington Branch, skirts the entire eastern and northern borders and approaches nearly to the western boundaries, and has been of such great importance to so large a portion of the people of the County, that a sketch of some of the results accomplished by the building of the road will be interesting.

The Metropolitan Branch of the Baltimore and Ohio Railroad was chartered in 1865, and completed and operated in the spring of 1873. The road runs diagonally through the County from its north-west corner to its south-eastern extremity, and is available to nearly every section of it, and when its Hanover Switch Branch is constructed, every neighborhood of the County will be within easy reach of either a railroad or canal.

Richard Randolph, Assistant Engineer, located the whole line, and was then transferred to Valley Road of Virginia.

James A. Boyd had the first contract, which was for section 11, Parr's Ridge, which is here 250 feet lower than the Parr's Ridge on Main Line; this was a deep cut three-fourths of a mile long, running from grade to 30 feet cut in one-fourth, then 30 feet for one-fourth of a mile, then running out in the next one-fourth of a mile. About the time this section was finished, several of the next heaviest were put under contract.

James A. Boyd took sections 10, 12, 13, 14, 15 and 16. Henry Gautz, 17, 18, 19 and 20. E. D. Smith, section 7, including the masonry of Bridge over Monocacy; the grade is 90 feet above low water over this stream; there is a very heavy embankment on west side, greatest height 70 feet; a long rock cut on east side, 20 to 30 feet deep for more than three-fourths of a mile.

The iron superstructure for this Monocacy Bridge was built by the Company, at their Mount Clare shops. Three spans of 200 feet each and one of 100. This one mile section cost, including graduation, masonry and bridge superstructure, $300,000. Sections 1, 2, 3, 4, including the Calico Rocks, were built by the Company's forces. Sections 5 and 6, by Bernard Riley. Sections 8 and 33, by Peter McNamara. Section 9, by White and McArdle. 21, Timothy Flaherty. 22 and 23, B. R. Codwise. 24, 25, 26, Michael Buoy. 27 and 30, Dennis Murphy. 28 and 29, Timothy Cavan. 31, 32 and 33, G. M. Watkins. 34 and 37, Patrick McCabe. 35, Alfred Ray. 36 and 39, James Forward. 40, Thomas A. Waters. 41 and 42, by Company's force.

Not finding materials for bridges at the crossing of Little Monocacy, Little and Big Seneca,—these streams were crossed on trestles, constructed by the Company's forces. Little Monocacy and Big Seneca, 70 feet high, and at Little Seneca, 106 feet high. The intention is to replace these trestles with permanent structures of stone and iron, when the trestles shall have been used to a proper extent.

The maximum grade is 50 feet per mile. Minimum radius of curvature, 1000 feet. Elevation at Gaithersburg, 516 feet above tide.

Distance from Point of Rocks to Baltimore by old line 69 miles.
   "      "      "      " via Washington new line 80   "

As the location of Washington seems to be on ground prepared for a site of the seat of Government of a great Nation, so Montgomery County seems prepared to furnish supplies of all kinds for the inhabitants of such a city; Milk, Butter, Poultry, Hay, Fruit and Vegetables, in fact, every thing which will not stand long carriage. Also, by means of this road, to furnish locations for country residences for those who can afford it, the whole line from Washington to Sugar Loaf Mountain furnishes sites for cottages, where abundant water of best quality, shade trees and soil most favorable for gardeners can be found.

All important passenger trains of the Baltimore and Ohio Company, including local and fast freight, pass over the Metropolitan Branch, affording unprecedented facilities to the people for personal travel and transportation of productions and supplies. There are twenty-eight stations on the road from Washington to Point of Rocks, or the Washington Junction, the intersection with the Main Stem, a distance of forty-two and one-half miles, viz:

METROPOLITAN BRANCH.

| *Stations.* | *Miles.* | *Stations.* | *Miles.* |
|---|---|---|---|
| Washington | 0 | Rockville | 16¼ |
| Metropolitan Junction | 1 | Derwood | 19 |
| Queenstown | 3¼ | Washington Grove | 20¾ |
| Terra Cotta | 4 | Gaithersburg | 21½ |
| Stott's | 4¼ | Clopper's | 24½ |
| Brightwood | 6¼ | Germantown | 26½ |
| Silver Springs | 7 | Little Seneca | 28½ |
| Linden | 9 | Boyd's | 29½ |
| Forest Glen | 9½ | Barnesville | 33¼ |
| Ray's Quarry | 9¾ | Dickerson | 35¾ |
| Knowles | 11 | Tuscarora | 39 |
| Windham's | 13½ | Sugar Loaf | 41¾ |
| Halpin | 15½ | Washington Junction | 42¾ |

The following is the list of Officers of the Road at present:

| | |
|---|---|
| *President* | J. W. Garrett. |
| *Vice-President* | John King, Jr. |
| *2d Vice-President* | Wm. Keyser. |
| *Chief Engineer* | James L. Randolph. |
| *General Freight Agent* | M. R. Smith. |
| *Master of Transportation* | W. M. Clements. |
| " " *Road* | John Bradshaw. |
| " " *Machinery* | John C. Davis. |
| *Treasurer* | W. H. Ijams. |
| *Auditor* | W. T. Thelin. |
| *Superintendent Pittsburg Division* | E. K. Hyndman. |
| " *Trans. Ohio Division* | C. H. Hudson. |
| *General Ticket Agent* | L. M. Cole. |
| *Supt. Terminal Tracks and Stations* | John L. Wilson. |

# CHAPTER XIII.

## PROMINENT MEN.

*Col. John Berry. Elisha Riggs. Samuel Riggs. Mrs. Ann Poultney. Philip E. Thomas. Rev. Reuben T. Boyd. His Ordination as Minister of the Gospel. His Certificate to perform marriage, signed by General Wm. Henry Harrison. John C. Clark. George R. Gaither. Israel H. B., and A. and R. R. Griffith. Thomas L. Reese. William Darne. Rev. Thomas McCormick. Thomas Moore. Caleb Bently. Isaac Riggs. Roger Brooke. Hon. Francis P. Blair. Robert Pottinger. Dr. Wm. Bowie Magruder. Major George Peters. Drs. Duvall. Tobacco Inspectors. Robert Sellman. Thos. B. W. Vinson, Triadelphia Cotton Factory.*

COL. JOHN BERRY, who participated in the defence of Fort McHenry when bombarded by the British in 1814, and whose well directed guns caused the British lion to weigh anchor and drop down the river, out of the reach of the artillery of the Fort. For his gallantry on this occasion he attracted the attention of Maj. Gen. Winfield Scott—by an offer of promotion and transfer to another important military post. He preferred, after successfully defending his adopted City, to return to private life, and devoted himself to the development of the patent fire brick with his brother, Mr. THOS. L. BERRY, in the south-east part of the City, which proved eminently successful and profitable. He accumulated a large fortune, leaving as his representatives, Gen. John Summerfield Berry, and John Hurst, the successful dry goods merchant and president of the National Exchange Bank.

ELISHA RIGGS, for many years the head of the well known firm of Riggs, Peabody & Co., on Baltimore street, near Hanover; afterwards Peabody, Riggs & Co., German street. The elder partner removed to New York, after aiding and establishing the well known firm of Corcoran & Riggs, of Washington. He died, leaving a fortune of a million and a half of dollars. Mr. George Peabody, at one time his clerk, afterwards his partner, had in the meantime removed to London, where, in his successful efforts to maintain and uphold the credit of Maryland, he laid the foundation of his own colossal fortune, a part of which, in his life-time, he devoted to the development of art and instruction for the benefit of the City of Baltimore, by the establishment of the magnificent institute, "The Peabody Institute," on Mount Vernon Place, which bears and will hand down down his name to generations yet unborn.

SAMUEL RIGGS the junior member of the firm died in early life, leaving a fortune of $300,000 dollars.

Mrs. ANN POULTNEY, relict of the late Charles Poultney, and sister of Philip E. Thomas, remarkable for her culture, piety and refinement, also as a prominent member and speaker of the Society of Friends.

PHILIP E. THOMAS, founder, and for many years the President of the Baltimore and Ohio Railroad,—the first commercial railroad undertaken in the United States.

The Rev. REUBEN T. BOYD, of this County, father of Col. T. H. S. BOYD, the publisher of this history, born July 3rd, 1794, on the old estate of the Boyd's, known as "Boyd's Delay," on Rock Creek, three miles east of Rockville. He studied for the ministry, and was authorized to preach the Gospel in the Baltimore District of the Methodist Episcopal Church, November 26th, 1825. His certincate being signed by Rev. Joseph Frye, President, James R. Williams, Secretary; renewed December 30th, 1826, signed Joseph Frye, President, and J. S. Reese, Secretary. For several years preceding and during this time a great reform was being agitated in the Methodist Episcopal Church, the object of which was a change in the form of government, so as to admit of the representatives of Lay members in the councils of the church.

Mr. Boyd took an active and zealous stand in behalf of the projected reform, and was a constant contributor to the columns of a pamphlet published by William Stockton, father of the late Rev. Thos. H. Stockton, one of the most eminent pulpit orators of his day, and Chaplain of the United States House of Representatives. This pamphlet was published in the interest of the reformers, and soon brought down on their devoted heads, the violent denunciation and abuse of the Bishops and Elders of the Church, which finally resulted in the expulsion of eleven Ministers for advocating the rights of the Laity. Reuben T. Boyd was the youngest of the eleven, and many amusing anecdotes are related of the Radicals, as they were called by their former associates. The controversy waxed warm, and shook the government of Methodism to its foundation. But the original eleven were not to be crushed; imbued with the fire and spirit that animated their forefathers, they soon gathered around them a strong following, and banded themselves together under the name of the Associated Methodist Churches, and at the Maryland Annual Conference of Ordained Ministers and Lay Delegates, held in Baltimore, April 5th, 1829, he was ordained for the office of Deacon, and authorized by the said Conference to administer the ordinance of Baptism; to assist the Elder in the administration of the Lord's Supper, to celebrate Marriage, and to preach and expound the Holy Scriptures, so long as his life and doctrine accord with the Gospel of our Lord Jesus Christ. Signed by Rev. Nicholas Snethen, President, and Luther J. Cox, Secretary.

Their organization rapidly increased, when they gave it the name of the Methodist Protestant Church, and at their Maryland Annual Conference of Ministers and Delegates, held in the City of Georgetown, District of Columbia, April the 8th, 1832, he was ordained for the office of Elder in the Methodist Protestant Church, and authorized by said Conference, so long as his life and doctrine accord with the Holy Scriptures, to administer the Lord's Supper, to Baptize, to celebrate Matrimony, and to feed the flock of God, taking oversight, not as a Lord over God's heritage, but being an example to the flock.

Signed by order and in behalf of the Maryland Annual Conference, Rev. Eli Henkle, President, James Hanson, Secretary. Mr. Henkle was the father of the present member of Congress from the Fifth Maryland District.

Their Church membership rapidly spread, and new Conferences formed especially in the South and West. Feeling that his sphere of usefulness would be enlarged by removing to the West, he was transferred to the Illinois Conference in 1838, and from there to the Ohio Conference in 1840, where he remained nine years.

The following certificate recorded in the Court of Common Pleas for Hamilton County, State of Ohio, and signed by General Harrison, Clerk of the Court, and afterwards President of the United States, will be of interest, showing as it does that General Harrison, at the time of his election to the Presidency, was Clerk of the Court of Hamilton County, Ohio.

"STATE OF OHIO, HAMILTON COUNTY, ss.:

"Be it known, that on the 28th day of November, in the term of November, A. D. eighteen hundred and forty, of the Court of Common Pleas, within and for said County, Reuben T. Boyd produced to said Court satisfactory evidence and credentials of his being a regular ordained Minister of the Methodist Protestant Church, in the Ohio Annual Conference, and now officiating as such on the Cincinnati Circuit. Whereupon the Court grant unto said Reuben T. Boyd, a License, authorizing him to solemnize Marriages throughout said State, agreeably to the requisitions of the Statute of said State, in such case made and provided, so long as he shall continue a regular Minister in said society or congregation.

"By order of Court.

"In testimony whereof, I have hereunto set my hand and affixed the seal of said County at Cincinnati, this the 28th day of November, A. D. 1840.

"WM. H. HARRISON, *Clk.*
"J. J. SNIDER, *Dep.*"

Endorsed on the back:

"Recorded in the Marriage Records of Logan County, Ohio, on the 4th day of April, 1844.

N. L. MCCOLLOCH, *Clerk.*

"Entered on the Records in the Clerk's office, Champaign County, March 28th, 1844.

SAMUEL H. ROBBINSON, *Clerk.*

"Entered on the Records in the Clerk's office, Union County, April 24th, 1844.

JOHN CASSIL, *Clerk.*"

He returned to the Maryland Conference in 1849, where he continued an active and efficient Minister, until 1859, when health failing him, he was placed on the the superannuated roll of the Conference. After an active and continuous life of thirty-four years in the Ministry, he was compelled to seek rest, and where should he look for this haven but in his native County, where the scenes of early childhood would recall the happy memories of his youth. He bought property in Clarksburg, and removed his family in 1859, where he lived to enjoy the remaining days of his life in the happy enjoyment of a consciousness of a bright future beyond the grave. He died seated in his easy chair, surrounded by his books and papers, on the 15th of February, 1865, in his seventy-second year. At peace with God and mankind, honored and respected by all, he left behind a record worthy of example. During his life he was a constant and voluminous writer, his publications in the Methodist Protestant and Western Recorder attracting universal attention.

JOHN C. CLARK, the well known Merchant and Banker, was born in Clarksburg, and in early youth removed to Baltimore, and engaged in business with more than ordinary success. He was very unfortunate in the death of his children; of a family of nine, all of whom, with one exception, attained adult age, and several married—he had buried all several years before his own death, which occurred in 1867, at the age of seventy-four. After providing well for his grandchildren, all of whom are now living in Baltimore, or its vicinity—and making other bequests, he bequeathed property to the value of half a million of dollars to a Beneficiary Society, which, at his instance, had been incorporated in connection with Saint John's Methodist Protestant Church in Liberty street, Baltimore, which is to occupy a magnificent site on Madison avenue, near the Park.

GEORGE R. GAITHER, recently deceased, one of Baltimore's most opulent citizens, left a fortune of one million three hundred thousand dollars, consisting of large and handsome stores and warehouses, on Baltimore, Hanover, German, Howard and Charles streets, and handsome dwelling houses on Cathedral street.

ISRAEL H. B., and A. and R. R. GRIFFITH, for many years flourished as successful Merchants of Baltimore. Upon the death of the first named, investments in stocks and bonds to the amount of four hundred and forty-five thousand dollars were found in a trunk under his bed.

THOMAS L. REESE, the father, and grandfather of the well known grocery firm, now doing business in Baltimore, was for a number of years a highly esteemed citizen of old Montgomery.

In early life he was a clerk with the celebrated Johns Hopkins, in the counting-room of their uncle Gerard T. Hopkins, and often has the great capitalist been heard to say, that when he came to Baltimore he had but five dollars in the world, but he had resolved to become a rich man.

When about twenty-five years of age he married Mary, daughter of Thomas Moore—and lived for six or eight years in Brookeville, engaged in mercantile life, filling several offices of honor and trust, everywhere esteemed as a conscientious and upright man.

From there he returned to Baltimore, and became a partner in the wholesale grocery firm of Gerard T. Hopkins & Co.

In 1833 he opened a retail store on Pratt street, desiring to educate his sons in all the details of the business, where he remained until 1844, when he retired from active life, but still by his daily counsel and advice, aiding his sons, who succeeded him, in building up the large business they are now doing.—In early life he was often heard to say that he never desired to become a rich man, and although actively engaged for more than thirty years in mercantile life, during which he reared and educated a large family, he died in moderate circumstances, but leaving to posterity a legacy more valuable than any amount of earthly riches,—*a good name.*

Among other names worthy of being mentioned is that of WILLIAM DARNE, of Mountain View, at the foot of the Sugar Loaf Mountain, who afterwards removed to Darnestown, where he died.

Mr. Darne was distinguished for his hospitality and urbanity of manners.   He left a family of daughters equally distinguished for beauty, culture, ease and elegance of manner.   One of whom married Capt. Smoot of the Navy; another, Capt. Lacy of the Army; another, Dr. Bell, a practising physician of the County.   Mr. Darne several times represented the County in the State Legislature and as a director in the Chesapeake and

7

Ohio Canal.   He also left one son, Mr. Alexander, Darne of the County.

Rev. THOMAS MCCORMICK was born in Loudoun County, Virginia, in 1792, but came to Montgomery at the age of six to live with his uncle, Thomas Moore.   In 1806 he went to Baltimore and learned the trade of house carpenter, and fifteen years afterwards built the house now owned by E. J. Hall, Esq., at Longwood, near Brookeville, which he afterwards purchased, and where he resided for fifteen years in enjoyment of the pleasant surroundings.   He is now nearly eighty-eight years of age.

The late THOMAS MOORE lived in Brookeville, and was the inventor of the first refrigerator ever made, in which Thomas McCormick carried the first butter to market.   It was patented in 1803, and at first was of small size, made for the purpose of carrying butter to market on horseback, as most of the marketing was carried in those days.   The refrigerator consisted of a cedar tub of oval form, and about eighteen or twenty inches deep, in this was placed a tin box, with the corners square, which would contain twenty-two prints of butter of one pound each, leaving space on each side, between the tin and wood, for ice in small lumps.   The outside of the wooden box was covered with rabbit skin with the fur on, and over that was a covering of coarse woolen cloth.   In this refrigerator the butter was carried on horseback to the market at Georgetown, a distance of twenty miles, in warm weather, hard and firm, and with ice enough left to give each purchaser a small lump.   This butter commanded a much higher price than any other.

Thomas Moore was a remarkable man.   His father, Thomas Moore, an Irish Quaker, came to this country early in the last century, settled first in Pennsylvania, where he married, and afterwards removed to Loudoun County, Virginia, where he built a residence and called the place Waterford, after his native home.   Here the son Thomas for a time carried on the business of a cabinet-maker, which he had learned.   He then engaged in milling and merchandising in connection with his brother-in-law, James McCormick.   About the year 1794 he removed to Maryland, having married Mary Brooke, daughter of Roger Brooke, of Brooke Grove, in Montgomery County.   Here he commenced farming on the estate of his wife, and soon distinguished himself as a practical farmer.

The State of Maryland is greatly indebted to him for many improvements in agriculture. Although the land was poor when he took possession of it, he soon had the model farm of the County and State. This farm is now owned by E. J. Hall, Esq., former President of the Montgomery County Agricultural Society, who married a niece of Mary Moore. Persons came from long distances to see his farm and witness the deep plowing with the mammoth plow of his own invention, his fine stock of cattle in fields of red clover, his meadows of timothy, fine fields of corn, the ground yellow with pumpkins, and the large pen of small bone hogs, fattened on pumpkins, corn and slop, boiled in a wooden box.

One of his distinguished visitors was Charles Carroll, son of Carroll of Carrollton, who came on purpose to see the farm and improvements. The proprietor being absent on that occasion, it devolved upon the twelve-year-old nephew to show the visitor around, which service was rewarded by the first silver dollar the farmer boy ever called his own.

Thomas Moore, about this time, wrote a treatise on agriculture, and another on ice-houses and refrigerators, which proved of signal benefit to the State of his adoption. In the year 1805, he was employed by the Corporation of Georgetown to construct the causeway from Mason's Island to the Virginia shore, for which he received twenty-four thousand dollars, and completed the work in less than one year. After this he was employed by the United States Government to lay out the great National Road to the West. During the war with Great Britain, from 1812 to 1816, he took charge of the Union Manufacturing Works, near Ellicotts' Mills, as chief manager.

About this time he, in connection with his two brothers-in-law, Caleb Bently and Isaac Biggs, purchased the site and erected the cotton mills known as Triadelphia, Montgomery County, Md. This was not a profitable investment, the war closing soon after the factory went into operation. He was next called upon by the Board of Public Works of the State of Virginia to accept the position of Chief Engineer of the James River Canal. He also served in the same capacity in the Chesapeake and Ohio Canal, where, after making considerable progress, he contracted a fever so fatal to many on the Potomac, and came home to end his life with his family. From the year 1818 until his death he occupied, with much honor to himself and with great benefit to the public, and with the entire approbation of those to whom he was responsible, the office of principal Civil Engineer of the State of Virginia. On the 3rd of October, after a sickness of twelve days, aged 63 years, he quietly departed this life like one falling into a quiet slumber.

ROGER BROOKE, an immediate descendant of one of the first settlers of the colony of Maryland, was noted for wit and humor, and though a Quaker, he had, like Washington, a great fondness for his hounds and the fox chase; and was one of the best, most active and successful farmers of the County. Mr. Francis P. Blair, in an agricultural address, characterized him as a second Franklin.

Mr. BLAIR above alluded to, who so beautifully and elegantly established himself at his well known seat of Silver Springs, was attracted to the spot under singular circumstances. He had purchased a very fine saddle horse, Selim, of the late Gen. Wm. Lingan Gaither, another of Montgomery's representative men, who had repeatedly served his native County with credit and ability in both branches of the State Legislature. In taking a ride with his daughter, beyond the limits of the District of Columbia and in the lower part of Montgomery County, Selim became frightened, threw his rider, and ran down among the thick growth of pines in the valley to the west of the road. Mr. Blair followed and found the horse fast to a bush, which had caught the dangling reins of the bridle. Near the spot he spied a bold fountain bubbling up, the beautiful white sand sparkling in the water like specks of silver. Mr. Blair became so charmed with the spot and the spring, that he resolved at once if possible to possess it. He sought its owner, and soon a bargain was made at what then was considered a good price by the seller; but in the eyes of Mr. Blair as very cheap. This led to the proprietorship of the far-famed and classic seat of Silver Springs; where its venerable and distinguished owner spent in elegant retirement the last twenty-five years of his long and eventful life, and died peacefully, full of years and full of honors, at the advanced period of eighty-five.

ROBERT POTTINGER and Dr. WILLIAM BOWIE MAGRUDER, father of the late most excellent and valuable citizen and physician, Dr. WM. B. MAGRUDER, of Brookeville, were leading and prominent citizens of the County, in their day and generation.

Major GEORGE PETER was a member of Congress for this District, and during life a prominent and active politician. He served in the Legislature of the State. He commanded an artillery company in the war of 1812, and had among his soldiers George Peabody, who subsequently became the great banker and philanthropist, and the late George R. Gaither of Baltimore, who then, with Mr. Peabody, resided in Georgetown, D. C.

The two Drs. DUVALL, father and son, were prominent and active in their professions, as politicians and representatives of the County in the State Legislature.

The different State Inspectors of Tobacco, appointed from Montgomery County, were Richard H. Griffith, Philemon Griffith, John W. Darby, Francis Valdemar, Perry Etchison, Greenberry S. Etchison, and the present popular Inspector, Robert S. Hilton.

ROBERT SELLMAN, of Montgomery County, was, before the repeal of the law, appointed State Flour Inspector. He so actively and faithfully discharged the duties of the office, that after the repeal of the law, he was, and still is continued as private inspector at the request of the merchants of Baltimore.

THOS. F. W. VINSON, well and favorably known to the citizens of Montgomery County, was a fine specimen of the gentlemen of the olden times. His pleasing manners at once put his friends, as well as strangers, at perfect ease in his presence. He was for many years Sheriff of the County, and one of the Judges of the Orphans' Court.

Mr. JAMES HOLLAND, grandfather of the present Thomas J. and Clagett Holland, was said strongly to resemble General Washington in his personal appearance. As an auctioneer, he was known far and near. A peculiarity of his habit was always to give ample notice to both seller and buyer. "Going, going, going, the last chance, *owners and bidders look out.*"

The principal manufacturing establishment in the County was Triadelphia Cotton Factory, founded in 1809, by three brothers-in-law, ISAAC RIGGS, THOMAS MOORE and CALEB BENTLY.

A Woolen Factory was established in the neighborhood about the same time by DAVID NEWLIN,—all members of the Society of Friends.

# CHAPTER XIV.

## PROMINENT MEN—CONTINUED.

*Hon. Geo. W. Hilton. Wm. Darne, of Mountain View. Prof. Benjamin Hallowell. Hon. Allen Bowie Davis. Edward Stabler. W. T. R. Saffell. Francis Cassott Clopper. William Wilson. Leonidas Wilson. Hon. Thomas Lansdale. Dr. Richard Waters. John S. Belt. Hon. Richard Waters, and others.*

WORTHY of mention among the self-made men of the County is the HON. GEORGE W. HILTON, born in Laytonsville, October the 2d, 1823, and educated in Georgetown, District of Columbia. Soon after completing his education he commenced the teaching of school in the old mountain school house, in the third district, afterwards he taught school in Clarksburg and Cracklin Districts. In 1847, he was appointed Deputy Sheriff and Collector, which position he occupied until he engaged in merchandising in Damascus, in 1852, where he successfully continued for seven years, when he purchased property in Clarksburg and removed there in 1859. By energy and enterprise, combined with strict business integrity, he succeeded in establishing a large and profitable business, which he conducted until 1872, when he turned his attention to agricultural pursuits. Having purchased four tracts of land adjacent to the village of Clarksburg, he set about renovating and improving them, by a liberal and judicious expenditure in lime and fertilizers, including grasses, he has succeeded in bringing them up to a degree of fertility that is amply repaying him for his expenditure.

Mr. Hilton's ability soon attracted the attention of the people, and he was called to the Legislature in 1869, and served the people in the session of 1870 so faithfully, that he was re-elected for a second term in 1872, serving on the committees of corporations and printing with marked ability. With a keen perception for the details of measures that affected the interests of the County, he was ever foremost in perfecting and pressing them to a favorable conclusion. He was also appointed by Gov. Carroll, in 1877, on the Board of Control and Review that had the revising of the tax assessments. Mr. Hilton finds ample opportunity for the display of his spirit of enterprise in the improvement and beautifying of his lands and tenements, having erected several handsome dwellings in Clarksburg, that have added materially in promoting the attractions of the village.

"Mountain View," the old home of William Darne, is a farm containing about 150 acres of land, watered by Little Monocacy on the north-east, and bounded on the south and south-west by the County roads leading from Barnesville to Maj. Hempston's Old Brick Mill. The lands of the Gotts and Plummers lie adjacent at the south, those of Abraham S. Hayes and Z. G. Harris on the east and south-east, and those of Colmore Offutt and Hanson Hays on the north. The proprietorship of some of these lands is now no doubt different. Patrick McDade's old mill was located on Little Monocacy, about half a mile north of Mountain View.

Prominent among those whose deeds have added lustre to the name and fame of the Friends' Society of Sandy Springs, and of Montgomery County, is that of BENJAMIN HALLOWELL, Philosopher, Philanthropist, Orator, Farmer and Teacher; gifted with an extraordinary variety of knowledge, prominent in the many fields of investigation, in which he exerted his powerful energies, and prosecuting his researches with one ultimate aim, the happiness of his fellow-creatures. He was born in Montgomery County, Pennsylvania, on the 17th of August, 1799, and came to Montgomery County, Maryland, in 1819, as Mathematical teacher at the Boarding School at Fair Hill, which was established in that year. In 1824, he established a school at Alexandria, Virginia, and received among his pupils, from all sections of the country, many who have since attained position and honor. The Rev. Mrs. R. T. Boyd, relict of the late Rev. R. T. Boyd, of this County, and mother of the publisher, attended his courses of lectures in Alexandria, in the years 1834 and '35. Mr. Hallowell came to live upon his farm " Rockland," near Sandy Springs, in the summer of 1842, this was a poor tract of land, but by judicious draining, fertilizing and grass seeding, it was completely reclaimed, and with the buildings of the Rockland Seminary, which he established, now under the control of his son, HENRY C. HALLOWELL, presents a beautiful and attractive appearance. In 1859, he was elected First President of the Maryland State Agricultural College. He was prominent in organizing the Farmers' Club of Sandy Springs, the first meeting of which was held at the residence of Richard T. Bently. He was a frequent lecturer before various associations on scientific and agricultural subjects. He was Professor of Chemistry in the Medical Department of Columbia College, Washington; a member of the American Philosophical Society of Philadelphia, and one of the foremost in the Baltimore Yearly Meeting, to adopt plans for the improvement of the condition of the Indians on the Western borders. He died in 1877, in the 78th year of his age, regretted and beloved by all that knew him.

Among the many improved estates in the County, is Greenwood, the residence of Hon. ALLEN BOWIE DAVIS. This place was purchased in 1755, by Ephraim Davis, the grandfather of the present owner, and by him transmitted to his son Thomas Davis, who during President Washington's administration, raised a company and marched to Pennsylvania in 1794, to suppress the "Whiskey Insurrection." He was elected to the State Legislature while thus engaged, and frequently thereafter filled the same position, he was also elector of the Senate under the old Constitution, and occupied numerous positions in the County, from Magistrate, Surveyor and Conveyancer to Judge of the County Court. He died in 1833, honored and regretted by a large circle of friends.

Mr. Davis, the present proprietor of Greenwood, began a long career of public duties and usefulness very early in life, succeeding his father in the Board of Trustees of the Brookeville Academy, at the age of twenty-four. In 1840, he was elected a member of the Board of Public Works of the State, in which he exercised his influence in favor of the representation of the minority, and the abolition of political agencies in the management of public trusts. In 1850, he was elected to the State Constitutional Convention, and was made one of the first trustees of the State Agricultural College, and subsequently President of the Board. At the same time, he was elected President of the Montgomery Manufacturing Company, of Triadelphia. He was also President of the Montgomery County Agricultural Association.

In 1849, he obtained the charter for the Brookeville and Washington Turnpike Company, was elected President, served sixteen years, completed the road and retired from the Company. In 1863, he was elected to the State Legislature, and in 1869 was elected President of the Maryland State Agricultural Society. In addition, he has taken an active interest in the works of internal improvement, of social and agricultural advancement, of national polity and other matters pertaining to the prosperity of the people of the County and State.

One of the oldest settlers now living in the County is EDWARD STABLER, who is eighty-five years of age. He has been Postmaster of Sandy Springs for fifty years, and is the oldest Postmaster in the United States. He was the originator of the Mutual Fire Insurance Company, of Montgomery County, which was organized in 1848; he was elected President, and still holds the office, enjoying the entire confidence of the Company and community.

The Hon. Allen Bowie Davis, in a speech at a meeting of the State Agricultural Society in 1876, said of this family, "That the farm—a part of which Mr. Asa Stabler occupies, was purchased about thirty years ago, by Caleb Stabler, father of Mr. Stabler, Jr.,—at $2.05 per acre, or $820 for 400 acres. It was then without house or fencing. Mr. S. not having a plethoric purse, built a comfortable two story log house, with other necessary outhouses of the same material, and called it Drayton. To Drayton he removed with his family, consisting of a wife, one daughter and four sons. He inclosed a garden, and planted a small orchard. His first crop of wheat was five bushels sown, from which he reaped two and a half bushels,—the first reward of his labor. Acting upon the maxim of an old Quaker progenitor—"if thee is kind to the land, it never will give thee an ungrateful return,"—he persevered, and did obtain a grateful and bounteous reward.

"Accepting an invitation to spend a night at Drayton, some years ago, I found the venerable patriarch and his no less venerable wife alone, and by them I was received with all the cordial but unostentatious and simple hospitality which it was possible for a host and hostess to lavish upon the most honored and distinguished guest. I soon learned from them that their daughter was married, and all of the sons grown up and settled out for themselves. After tea, a rap at the door announced a visitor, and one by one the four sons and the son-in-law came in to inquire after the health of father and mother, and to pay their respects to their guest. I learned also, that the 400 acres had been divided into six parts, and that each of the sons and son-in-law had built and was settled on his portion—the old folks retaining the homestead—and that each was near enough, after the labor of the day and after tea, to walk over to Drayton, to inquire after the well-being of their parents. I thought I never saw a brighter or happier family, or witnessed a more interesting or so instructive a scene.

"Within a few days past I have again passed through the same original farm, now cut up and divided, as already stated. The venerable sire and his consort still survive; each of the sons and son-in-law are in genteel and comfortable houses, surrounded with well kept gardens and orchards, flowers, shrubs and ornamental trees and farm,—as Mr. Stabler can testify— yielding from 26 to 32 bushels of wheat per acre, with corresponding crops of corn, hay and straw, supplemented by all varieties of fruit, from the early strawberry to October peach and hard russet apple."

Mr. W. T. R. SAFFELL, was born September 18th, 1818, two miles south of Barnesville, on a farm called Knott's Place, where his father Lameck Saffell resided. He was baptised by Rev. Mr. Green, and first heard the Gospel preached by Rev. Basil Barry. His great uncle was Charles Saffell, a revolutionary soldier and pensioner, who lived on a farm five miles north of Rockville, near Gaithersburg, and died in 1837, at the age of ninety. At the beginning of the revolution, he lived with his father, a French musician, in Prince George's County. From that County he marched to Annapolis and joined the Regiment of the Maryland Flying Camp, under the command of General Rezin Beall, and sailing to the head of Elk River, he marched north to New York in the company commanded by John Hawkins Lowe. Charles was a drummer, fifer and bugler at the battles of Long Island, Fort Washington, Brandywine, Germantown and Monmouth. In his latter days he was an Auctioneer, and in that capacity visited all parts of the County. As a violinist, he amused himself in his feeble old age, and often reproduced the melodies of the Revolution in a peculiar style, now forever lost.

FRANCIS CASSOTT CLOPPER was born in Baltimore, July 26th, 1786; began life in Philadelphia, and when only eighteen years of age was sent by his employers to New Orleans, to collect moneys due them there, and at intermediate points. The trip was made on horseback, through a wild frontier country, alone, or with such chance companions as he might meet upon the road. His mission was successful, and he brought back the money quilted in his vest; after which he made many more trips like it.

On the 8th of July, 1811, he was married to Ann Jane Byrne, of Philadelphia, and in the following year he purchased the farm in Montgomery County, upon which he resided until his death,—the family having removed there in the same year,— making a continuous residence of fifty-seven years.

The original grants of the tracts of lands, comprised in the purchase, date back to 1748, to the times of the Lords Proprietary, and formed part of their Manor of Conococheague, or, as one of them has it, of "Calverton." The lands are described as lying upon "Sinicar" Creek, near the ford known as the "Indian Ford;" and it is said that the old Indian road from Washington to Frederick crossed Seneca a few yards above the present County road crossing.

The land at one time belonged to the Benson family, but about 1804 was sold to Zachariah McCubbin, from whom Mr. Clopper purchased it. Other tracts were bought from other parties at a later date. The original foundation of the mill is not known. One was standing in 1812 upon the site of the present saw-mill.

His public spirit was a prominent feature of Mr. Clopper's character,—always interested in some project for the advancement of the County.

The last twenty years of his life were expended, almost entirely, in efforts to procure the construction of a railroad through the County. At one time in the organization of the original Metropolitan Railroad Company, and when that failed in the business depression of 1857, he called the attention of the President of the Baltimore and Ohio Railroad to the advantages of the route to his company, and procured a reconoissance to be made, and a report, which later were followed up by the construction of the road.

Mrs. Clopper died in 1865, after a married life of fifty-four years, and Mr. Clopper in 1868,—the desire of his life, to see the Metropolitan Railroad completed, unsatisfied.

WILLIAM WILSON was born on the tract of land known as "Wilson's Inheritance," near the division line between Montgomery and Frederick Counties, on the left of the present road from Hyattstown to Barnesville. The tract is now owned by the Hershey family, John Sellman, and others. Jonathan Wilson, the grandfather of William, became the owner of this tract over one hundred years ago, was a member of the State Legislature when the County was first formed. He was a man of powerful constitution and lived to be ninety-eight years old; his death, at that age, resulting from accident.

He was a man of much intelligence, energy of character, and influence. His only son, John, inherited the estate, and lived in the house now occupied by Mr. C. R. Hershey. He also lived to an advanced age, ninety-three.

John had four sons, and a daughter who married Dr. Magruder, and became the mother of the late Dr. William B. Magruder, near Brookeville, and of other children—ten in all—whose descendants are numerous and widely scattered.

The eldest, John, lived and died on the paternal acres, a highly esteemed gentleman of the olden times, and a bachelor. He died in 1849, aged eighty-nine.

The second son, Thomas P., settled in Rockville, was for many years a prominent merchant there, and died at that place about the year 1832. His descendants are now living in Frederick City and County.

The fourth son, Charles, lived for many years in Medley's District, first as a merchant at Poolesville, then on a farm which he purchased, not far from the mouth of the Monocacy—the farm is now owned by the White family—and finally removed to the southern part of Kentucky, where he died. His descendants are to be found in Tennessee, Virginia, and Baltimore County of this State.

The third, William, very early in life, engaged in merchandising in Clarksburg, and continued the business uninterruptedly at the same stand for about forty-five years—dying in 1859, at the age of eighty-three. He married the eldest daughter of John Clark, one of the oldest residents of the village, (which was named after him,) and to his business, on his death, he succeeded.

Mr. LEONIDAS WILSON, his son, is still living, and resides in Clarksburg, and has accumulated a considerable fortune.

The Hon. THOMAS LANSDALE was born in this County in 1808. He was extensively engaged in mechanical operations for a number of years, and invented the first wood planing machine, and the metallic yoke for swing bells. In 1842, he became interested in the Triadelphia Mills, remaining five years, when he took charge of the Granite Factory at Ellicott's Mills, where he remained ten years. He was the first to introduce steam into a factory for heating purposes. In 1856, he returned to Triadephia, and by his enterprise and energy succeeded in making it a thriving village containing four hundred inhabitants, with a large three story stone Cotton Factory, Saw, Plaster, Bone and Grist Mills, Stone and Mechanical Shops. He was a member of the State Constitutional Convention of 1864, and was elected to the Senate 1865. He died in 1878, universally respected by the large circle of operatives, business men and politicians, with whom he was associated, while he lived in the confidence and esteem of his friends and neighbors.

JOHN THOMAS, who sixty years ago lived about six miles from Triadelphia, near Green's Bridge over the Patuxent, established an interesting industry for the collection of pine sap from the pine trees in the adjacent forests. This was done by removing a small chip from the foot of the tree, near the root, the opening thus made would receive the falling sap, which was gathered in the morning, taken to Mr. Thomas, who paid ten cents an ounce for it; the revenue derived from this source was not sufficient to meet the expectations of the projector, and it was abandoned; and the ancient Sap Tappers of the Patuxent is a tradition of the past.

Dr. RICHARD WATERS, of revolutionary fame, was born about 1760, and served as a Surgeon in the war for independence, and was noted for his skill as a surgeon as well as a practising physician. After the close of the War, he purchased a large estate called "Spring Garden," on the road leading from Goshen to Gaithersburg, and the road from Mechanicsville to Clarksburg. Dr. Waters was born in Prince George's County, where he married Miss Margaret Smith, by whom he had several children. His son Richard was a prominent man in the County, and held the office of Sheriff, while his brother Somerset was a prominent Commission Merchant of Baltimore, and served a long time as Tobacco Inspector.

JOHN S. BELT, a Justice of the Peace, of Clarksburg, married a grand-daughter of Dr. Waters. Mr. Belt is a young and efficient Magistrate, and takes a lively interest in the improvement of the social, intellectual and agricultural advancement of the County. He is Treasurer of the Clarksburg Literary Association, of which he is an active and efficient member. He is also extensively engaged in the fertilizing business, and his farm gives ample evidence of the benefits derived from skilful cultivation. He has recently planted an extensive orchard, containing choice varieties of fruit.

Hon. RICHARD WATERS, son of Dr. Richard Waters, of revolutionary fame, was born December 19th, 1794, on the old homestead, "Spring Garden," and at an early age took an active interest in the politics of the County. In his canvass for the legislative assembly, he found a great many young men who could neither read nor write, and, on investigation, he discovered that the money appropriated by the State for paying the tuition of those whose parents were unable to pay for the schooling of their children, was often used by the board of trustees, as they were called, in paying for children whose parents were able to pay, but their political influence was such as to enable them to divert the moneys intended for the instruction of the poor, to the payment of the education of their own children.

This led Mr. Waters to make a spirited canvass of the County, and he was elected to the Legislature by an overwhelming majority. One of his first efforts in the legislative assembly was for a change in the old system of school education, and he succeeded in having a bill passed for Public School Education in the State of Maryland, that resulted in the abolishment of the old system and inaugurated a new era in the education of the people. It was the initial movement, which has, by improvement, resulted in the present School System.

He was re-elected for a second term, and filled the position with honor, both to himself and his constituents. He is still living, and is about eighty-five years old. He has four sons and one daughter living.

His son Lemuel is an eminent divine in the Missouri Conference of the Methodist Episcopal Church, South.

William is the Agent of the Adams Express Company, in Cincinnati, Ohio.

Somerset is a Physician of large practice in Carroll County, and has served in the Legislature several terms from that County.

George still resides in the County, near the old ancestral acres, and has occupied several public offices of trust in the County.

Rebecca, the daughter, married Jesse T. Higgins, of this County, formerly a prominent merchant of Poolesville, and now a merchant of Baltimore.

The following names of citizens and families of the County are worthy of record, and of being handed down to posterity and honorable recollection, William Darne, Dr. S. N. C. White, William Pool, Abraham S. Hayes, William Bennett, Brook Jones, Joseph I. Johnson, Nathan Hempston, Jacob Nicholls, Horatio Trundle, Hezekiah Trundle, Richard Harding, William Trail, Thos. C. Lannan, Rev. Thos. W. Green, Dr. Horatio Wilson, Rev. Basil Barry, the Fletchers, Dawsons, Platers, Whites, Waters, Darbys, Gittings, Gotts, Glaizes, Kings, Purdums, Gaithers, Gues, Browns, Bensons, Brewers, Gassaways, Pooles, Neills, Huttons, Riggs, Owens, Gartrells, Perrys, Bealls, Dorseys.

# CHAPTER XV.

*Boundaries of the County. Building Stone. Roofing Slate.
Gold. Chrome. Quantity of Land and its Value. Number of
Horses and other Cattle. Farm Productions for 1878. Intellectual, Social and Agricultural Institutions. Population from
1790 to 1870. Society of Friends. Improvements at the close
of the Internecine War. Influence of the Metropolitan Railroad.*

MONTGOMERY COUNTY is bounded on the south-west by Virginia, from which it is separated by the Potomac River. The
Chesapeake and Ohio Canal runs along the whole south-western
boundary, following the banks of the Potomac River from
Georgetown to the mouth of the Monocacy. On the north-west
by Frederick County, being divided from it by a line running
from the mouth of Monocacy to Parr's Spring, on the Patuxent
River. On the north-east by Howard County, from which it is
separated by the Patuxent River. On the south-east by Prince
George's County, and south by the District of Columbia.

A red sandstone is found on the Potomac, near Seneca Creek,
and is known as the "Seneca Stone," and has been extensively
used in the District of Columbia,—the Smithsonian Institution,
in Washington, and many other buildings, both public and private, being built from these quarries.

A blue stone, of a bright color, and in every respect equal to
granite, is now being quarried on the Potomac River. The new
Georgetown College has been built from this stone, which can
be cut and finished into any shape; and, as a building stone,
for durability and beauty, has no equal in this section of the
country. It is also extensively used for foundation and paving
purposes, giving universal satisfaction.

Roofing slate is obtained in the vicinity of Hyattstown, and
is in extensive demand.

Gold is found in sufficient quantities, near the Great Falls of
the Potomac, to attract the attention of capitalists, who are

organizing for the successful operation of the mines, with a favorable prospect of success. A manufacturing jeweler, and his son, of Washington, make weekly excursions to the locality, and in the small streams of water, pick up sufficient ore in a few hours, in small lumps, ranging in size from a marble to that of an egg, which, upon smelting, will yield from eight to ten dollars worth of pure gold.

Chrome is also to be found in considerable quantities in different sections of the County.

Montgomery County contains two hundred and forty-two thousand three hundred and fifty-six acres, as follows: Improved—one hundred and sixty-two thousand one hundred and forty-three acres. Woodland—sixty-three thousand six hundred and sixty-six acres. Other unimproved land—sixteen thousand five hundred and forty-seven acres. Present cash value: Farms—five millions four hundred and eighty thousand five hundred and seventy-five dollars. Farming implements and machinery—three hundred thousand dollars. Annual amount of wages, including board—five hundred thousand dollars. Total amount of all farm productions, including improvements and additions to stock—two million dollars. Value of all live stock—one million of dollars. Number of horses—five thousand three hundred and sixty-four. Mules—four hundred. Milch cows—five thousand two hundred and twelve. Oxen—six hundred. Other cattle—five thousand. Sheep—six thousand nine hundred. Swine—fourteen thousand. Production of Wheat for the past year—three hundred and ten thousand bushels. Rye—thirty thousand. Corn—six hundred and forty thousand. Oats—one hundred and seventy-five thousand. Buckwheat—one thousand. Tobacco—six hundred and fifty thousand pounds. Wool—twenty thousand pounds. Potatoes—two hundred thousand bushels. Butter—two hundred and ten thousand pounds. Hay—thirteen thousand tons. Honey—three thousand four hundred and fifty pounds.

Among the Institutions which have rendered Montgomery County conspicuous for intellectual culture, and social and agricultural progress, are the

MONTGOMERY COUNTY AGRICULTURAL SOCIETY, organized in 1844. John C. Peter was the first President; A. B. Davis,

8

second; Robert P. Dunlap, third; Joseph H. Bradley, fourth; Elisha J. Hall, fifth; and John H. Gassaway, the present.

THE MUTUAL FIRE INSURANCE COMPANY of Montgomery County was chartered in 1848, with fifty thousand dollars worth of insurance. It has insured about nineteen million dollars worth of property during the thirty years of its existence, and has paid out for losses, by fire, over four hundred and fifty thousand dollars. They now hold policies of insurance on nearly fourteen million dollars worth of property; its operation extending to every County in the State. Robert R. Moore has served the Company as Secretary and Treasurer, from the beginning to the present time.

The ROCKVILLE MUTUAL BUILDING ASSOCIATION, the first institution of the kind in the County, was chartered in March, 1873.

CIRCULATING LIBRARIES are at Brookeville, Sandy Springs, Rockville, Poolesville and Darnestown.

The BROOKEVILLE, ROCKVILLE and DARNESTOWN ACADEMIES, are long established Institutions; also, the ROCKLAND SEMINARY, at Sandy Springs.

The Montgomery County Branch of the Prisoners' Aid Society. The Farmers' Club, of Sandy Springs; the Enterprise Farmers' Club; the Montgomery Farmers' Club; the Sandy Springs Lyceum; the Horticultural Society; the Home Interest Society and Young Folks' Sociable,—all of Sandy Springs.

The SANDY SPRINGS SAVINGS BANK was chartered in 1868, and has over eighty thousand dollars on deposit, largely from the laboring class. There are twenty-six Directors, who are among the most prominent and responsible citizens of the County. The funds of the Institution have been so well managed and invested, that the Bank, after paying all expenses, has annually paid to its depositors six per cent. on their deposits, reserving a surplus to meet contingencies. Caleb Stabler, President, B. Rush Roberts, Treasurer, and Allen Farquhar, Secretary.

Conspicuous in the work of intellectual, social and agricultural organization and development, are the GRANGERS of the County. They have thriving Lodges at Bethesda, Barnesville, Brighton, Damascus, Darnestown, Gaithersburg, Great Falls, Olney, Hyattstown and Liberty Grove.

The CLARKSBURG LITERARY ASSOCIATION, established in 1879, C. R. Murphy, President, William R. Windsor, Vice-President, John S. Belt, Treasurer, T. H. S. Boyd, Corresponding Secretary, and Thos. A. Burdette, Recording Secretary.

Montgomery County has witnessed three phases of civilization since the early settlements.

First, were the old Tobacco Planters, with their baronial estates and armies of slaves. They felled the native forests, and planted the virgin soil in tobacco and Indian corn. This did very well so long as there was timber for the axe, and new land for the hoe; and these old lords of manors were happy; they feasted, and frolicked and fox hunted, and made the most of life; those days are known as "the good old times."

In less than a century after this system of denuding and exhaustion began, there were no more forests to clear, and no more new land to till. Then succeeded the period of old fields, decaying worm fences, and mouldering homesteads. This sad condition of the County had reached its climax about the year 1840, the population of the County having steadily diminished from 1790, when it was eighteen thousand, down to fifteen thousand, when it was at its minimum, in this year, as will be seen by examining the census of the County.

## POPULATION OF THE COUNTY.

|  | WHITE. | COLORED. | TOTAL. |
|---|---|---|---|
| 1790 | 11,679 | 6,324 | 18,003 |
| 1800 | 8,508 | 6,550 | 15,058 |
| 1810 | 9,731 | 8,249 | 17,980 |
| 1820 | 9,082 | 7,318 | 16,400 |
| 1830 | 12,103 | 7,713 | 19,816 |
| 1840 | 8,766 | 6,690 | 15,456 |
| 1850 | 9,435 | 6,425 | 15,860 |
| 1860 | 11,349 | 6,973 | 18,322 |
| 1870 | 13,128 | 7,434 | 20,563 |

From 1790, there was a constant stream of emigration from the County, some going to the cotton fields of the South, but most to the fertile new lands of the West, including Kentucky and Missouri. Few of the enterprising young men settled on their fathers' farms.

The land would no longer yield an increase, and they made no attempt at renovating and improving the soil, and Montgomery lands became a synonym for poverty. The lands bordering the Rockville and Georgetown Turnpike, the then only paved road in the County, were with the exception of Robert Dick's, and one or two other farms, but a succession of uninclosed old fields. This was not universally the fact. The red lands of Medley's, and those around Brookeville, and in the Friends' Settlement at Sandy Springs, and on the Hawlings' River, with an occasional farm in other sections, had retained comparative fertility.

This emigration was not however in vain; it added strength and intelligence to the movement, which from the first settlement of the County, has ever been in progress from the Atlantic to the Pacific, and furnished representative men to other States.

The LAMARS of the South, who now have a representative in the United States Senate, and the grandfather of Thomas Benton, of Missouri, were from this County.

The late Senators, EDWARDS, of Illinois, with DAVIS and PROCTOR KNOTT, of Kentucky, besides a host of others who have filled distinguished positions at the bar, on the bench, and in every representative capacity throughout the Western States, were natives of this County.

The SOCIETY of FRIENDS, in the vicinity of Sandy Springs, who formed their settlement in the course of the decade preceding and following the middle of the eighteenth century, and who at every period of the history of the County have done so much to promote the material development and intellectual advancement of the County, first abandoned this destructive system of cultivation during the last quarter of the past century, induced thereto, by the change then made in the character of their labor.

The same society about 1845, introduced in this County the old Chincha Island, Peruvian Guano, the effect of which was magical. As soon as the people became aware that by the application of this new fertilizer to their old worn out lands, they could be made to produce remunerative crops of cereals and grasses; then they turned to their cultivation with the wonted energy of the race. This industry was greatly promoted by the Crimean war, which caused a material enhancement in the prices of all kinds of farm products.

From this epoch the cereal growing period may be dated—old buildings were renovated and repaired, while new buildings, and handsome residences, replete with modern improvements, took the place of the old tumble down, moss-covered, and worm-eaten cot of the past. New post and rail fences, with improved gates, replaced the old worm and picket fence, and the fields teemed with bountiful harvests. The decade from 1850 to 1860, was one of universal prosperity to the people of the County. Towns and villages sprung up, stores were established at cross roads, while internal improvements were progressing in all parts of the County.

Then came the dark spectre of Internecine War between the sections of the country, with its fair possessions filled with bitter dissensions and sectional differences, with all their blighting and devastating horrors. Again the young men sought the tented field, and the business of farming was, in many localities, suspended. Houses and fences were destroyed, and farms laid waste, by the marching and counter-marching of armies and the general ravages of war. Slavery was abolished during the war, and at its close the third era, or free labor period, was entered upon by the people.

The young men returned to their homes, with muscles hardened and energies quickened by their martial experience. They accepted with cheerfulness the new order of things, and fully alive to the kindly properties of their native soil, and acquainted with the means of rendering it productive, went to work with a will, and since that time every vestige of that unfortunate struggle has been effaced; and now, with a larger and increasing population, the people are making rapid strides towards an advanced state of enlightenment and material prosperity. Fine and imposing buildings are being erected, with beautiful lawns and gardens attached. Magnificent and substantial churches have taken the place of the old log meeting-houses, and are more numerous and largely attended. School houses, of superior construction, have greatly multiplied, and the school system more thorough and efficient than any which preceded it. The roads have been increased and improved, while handsome and substantial bridges span the creeks and water-courses, facilitating travel and transportation. The old fields have all been reclaimed, and under improved fencing, are yielding handsome returns to their owners.

The opening of the METROPOLITAN RAILROAD has exerted a marked influence upon the material improvement and prosperity of the County. Over half a million of dollars annually has been expended by the people in the purchase of lime, bone, phosphates and other fertilizers of a like character, resulting in the production of from eighteen to fifty bushels of wheat, and from thirty to sixty bushels of corn to the acre, giving employment to over thirty Mills, located on the various branches and streams in the County, several of which are Merchant Mills. Besides this, a large amount of grain is anually exported to Georgetown and Baltimore.

Market gardening and fruit growing are becoming extensive industries, and can nowhere else be more successfully prosecuted, the soil yielding abundantly, and of the best quality, all the vegetables and fruits common to a temperate climate.

The cultivation of the grape for the manufacture of wine is also growing into quite a business, and cannot fail to eventually prove successful, as this County is the home of many varieties of the wild grape, and the native soil of the Catawba. These various industries combined with the energy and enterprise of the people, must soon place the County in the foremost rank of Agricultural progress. The local advantages of this County are numerous, especially is this so, as regards the numerous rivers, streams and creeks that traverse every portion of the County, affording ample facilities for water-power, which, in the future, will be sure to promote and accelerate the march of improvement. The Great Falls on the Potomac is the largest available water-power in the world, and with its development and utilization for manufacturing purposes, cannot fail to eventuate in the growth of a considerable manufacturing town at that point.

The commercial importance of Baltimore, connected as it is with this County by the Baltimore and Ohio and Metropolitan Railroads, must exert a strong influence in the future progress and improvements of the County, being the great market from whence are drawn the supplies of Merchandise, Agricultural

Implements, Fertilizers, etc., demanded for the use and benefit of the County.

But above all, the influence of the National Capital which over-shadows but to bless this favored section of the land, must, in the near future, make this County all that its most sanguine people could wish or hope. Already many persons of distinction and wealth, whose business or inclination attracts them to Washington, are seeking sites for country villas or suburban residences.

# PRESENT OFFICERS OF THE COUNTY.

*Chief Judge*......................Hon. RICHARD J. BOWIE.

*Associate Judges*............... { Hon. JOHN W. LYNCH, Hon. W. VEIRS BOUIC.

*Clerk*...........................E. B. PRETTYMAN.

*Judges of Orphans' Court*....... { EDWARD W. OWEN, Dr. A. H. SOMMERS, SAMUEL DARBY.

*Register of Wills*................ROBERT W. CARTER.

*Commissioners*........... { 1st District, DAVID GRIFFITH, 2nd " JOSEPH HENDERSON, 3rd " W. W. POOLE, 4th " JOHN SAUNDERS, 5th " THOS. HARDESTY.

*Clerk*...........................JOS. A. TANEY.

*Sheriff*..........................JOHN AMBROSE CLEMENTS.

*Surveyor*........................WILLIAM GRADY.

*Board of School Commissioners*........ { SAMUEL JONES, WILLIAM T. JONES, WALTER M. TALBOT.

*Examiner and Treasurer*........Captain JAMES ANDERSON.

*State Senate*....................Hon. GEORGE PETER.

*Legislature*................ { Hon. MONTGOMERY BLAIR, Hon. HOWARD GRIFFITH, Hon. WILLIAM M. CANBY.

*State's Attorney*.................SPENCER C. JONES.

# CHAPTER XVI.

## APICULTURE—PEACH CULTURE.

*Keeping and Propagation of Bees. Process of removing Honey, without destroying Bees. Principal Bee Raisers in the County. Peach Trees. Propagation of Trees. List of desirable varieties.*

THE keeping and propagation of Bees in the County is assuming considerable importance. It requires but small capital and a very limited amount of muscular labor, while attended with little or no risk.

Bee keeping has become a science, and those who patiently learn their ways, have no fear of being stung. Neither are whole swarms of these industrious little creatures destroyed in order to secure their treasures of sweetness. On the contrary, they have really become pets of those who take a loving care of them.

To such perfection has the art of raising honey been brought, that, not a bee is sacrificed in taking away the honey, while the comb is even saved.

By a new and very ingenious little machine, the fresh combs when taken from the hives are deftly unsealed, and the honey extracted from the comb on the principle of suction by air, and the comb perfectly uninjured is returned to the hive to be filled again in a few days by the same bees. This honey is the purest known on the market, and is put up in sealed glasses, and is every day becoming a more staple article of food.

The feeding and keeping of bees is very easily learned, and is said by those engaged in it to be a most delightful employment. Two hundred and fifty dollars will stock a yard of bees, that with proper care will yield yearly one thousand dollars.

Mahlon T. Lewis, of Clarksburg, and Capt. F. P. Meigs, of Boyd's Station, are extensively engaged in their propagation.

Capt. Meigs purchased a handsome site at " Boyd's," and erected a magnificent residence, which was completed in 1879. The design is very attractive, embracing both the French,

English and Swiss styles of architecture, including the English basement, surmounted by a Swiss cottage roof with dormer windows; the building being heated by hot air, and illuminated by electricity. The grounds are beautifully laid out in the style of landscape gardening, containing all the varieties of fruits, including a vineyard, apiary and aviary.

Owing to the destruction of Peach trees by insects on the Peninsula, the Peach like the Tobacco Plant, must continually seek new land, since soil that has been planted in Peach trees, cannot be successfully replanted until it has been allowed a rest of many years. This will eventuate in the transfer from the Eastern Shore of the Peach culture, to the uplands of Montgomery, Frederick and Washington Counties.

The following extract from an article written expressly for the "Baltimore Sun," by Col. T. H. S. Boyd, describing the culture of the Peach and the propagating the scions, by the system of hybridizing, and a description of the popular varieties now in use, will be of interest.

"In the culture of the Peach the most approved method of propagating the 'scions' or young trees for the peach orchard is to procure the seed of the natural peach, as trees reared from it are better able to withstand the rigors of a hard winter, and and are much less liable to those diseases which, despite the best efforts of the grower, are always incidental to the system of 'hybridizing.' The seed are bedded in the early autumn, about six or eight inches below the surface of the ground, in a position exposed to the sun, so that by alternate freezing and thawing the hard resinous substance that holds the walls of the pit together, becomes softened and the kernel is easily extracted.—About the first of April, these kernels are planted in the nursery, about six inches apart, in rows four feet wide.

"As soon as the scions shoot about six inches above the ground, they are cultivated with hoe and harrow, after the same fashion as corn. In June, the largest and most thrifty scions are budded for transplanting from the nursery to the orchard in the fall. The others are budded in September for transplanting in the spring. They are usually budded on the north side of the tree, in order to prevent the bud being killed by the heat of the sun. The bud is inserted into the scion by crucially incising the bark of the stock a few inches above the ground, turning back the corners of the bark, and setting into the aperture thus formed between the sap and the bark a bud selected from a healthy tree, of that variety of peach which it is desired to propagate.

"This bud is secured in its place by turning back the bark and binding the incised parts with a tie of the inner bark of the basswood or a piece of common candlewick. In a week or ten days the nurseryman is able to determine what buds have become set or 'taken' and are incorporated with the stock. The binding is then removed and the scion thoroughly trimmed below where the bud has been set.

"The scion is again trimmed in the spring, both above and below the bud, and about the first of June, the top is cut off at an angle of 45 degrees about an inch above the bud, which has now become the largest branch of the scion. During the summer it is kept cultivated and trimmed, and is ready for transplanting to the orchard, the bud having united with the scion and the place where the scion was cut off no longer being noticeable.

"The orchard is now plowed, harrowed and fertilized, and crossed out for the young trees, which are usually placed sixteen feet apart in the rows, running east and west, and twenty-four feet apart in the rows running north and south.

"After the trees are planted they are well cultivated by plowing and harrowing, the furrows being thrown towards the roots of the trees, the operation being repeated every fortnight from April to August. The trees are carefully trimmed, and kept clear of broken twigs and branches, and as they advance in age are 'headed in' as it is termed, by lopping the large branches when new shoots form.

"The trees bear in the fourth year. A first-rate orchard, well cultivated, will yield a profit of about $100 an acre, if the fruit is handled judiciously.

"Out of the hundred or so varieties cultivated in the United States some nineteen or twenty are favored here. They are given below in the order of their ripening for market:

"1. The Beatrice, an ordinary and poorly flavored peach, only valued for its early maturity, starts the market about the middle of July.

"2. Hale's Early, a once quite popular peach, ripens about July 25th.

"3. Hollis' Early, a small peach, ripening about August 1st, and valued for its capacity for transportation.

"4. Walters' Early, or Mountain Rose, earliest of all varieties of red peach, beautiful in color and delicious in flavor, matures about August 5th.

"5. Early York, superseded almost entirely by former, ripens about August 7th.

"6. Crawford's Early, color a rich yellow with deep blush, regarded by many as the finest of all peaches, matures about August 10th.

"7. Mary's Choice, August 15th.

"8, 9, 10 and 11. The Druid Hill, Harkins' Seedling, Old Mixon Free, and Stump the World, all ripen about the same time, August 17th or 18th. The Mixon was once regarded as the finest of all freestone peaches, and a standard of peach values.

"12. Crawford's Late, a rich yellow, the best of all canning peaches, except the late Heath Cling; matures about August 20th.

"13. Jaques, is a yellow, very large and delicious peach, ripening about the same time, as do also,

"14 and 15. The Monmouth Melacaton and Susquehanna or Griffith, both large, rich, yellow fruit.

"16. The Magnum Bonum follows.

"17. The Late Heath Cling-stone, the most deliciously flavored of all the varieties, matures about September 12th. They are very abundant, and are all consumed for canning and preserving.

"18. Bear's Smock, is about the latest peach as yet successfully cultivated in this region; but there is,

"19. Solway's Late, which promises to do well.

" When this last variety is harvested the peach season is ended, but the fruit growers are endeavoring to obtain other varieties to extend the season still further. There are several new varieties which give promise of success in this direction, notably Fisher's Favorite, Cameron's Late Yellow, and Levy's Yellow Cling, all remarkably fine fruit, and, should they thrive, the peach season will no doubt be protracted till the middle or last of October, about a month longer than heretofore. So if the Andrews' and Alexander Early are also successful, the season will be very notably extended."

# CHAPTER XVII.

## THE WASHINGTON GROVE CAMP GROUND.

*Incorporators. Objects. Location. Present and Past Officers.*
*Cottages. Tents. Owners.*

THE WASHINGTON GROVE CAMP MEETING ASSOCIATION of the District of Columbia and Maryland, was chartered March 30th, 1874, by the State Legislature, with F. Howard, Wm. R. Woodward, J. T. Mitchell, B. H. Stinemetz, Th. Somerville, J. W. Wade, M. G. Emery, Alex. Ashley, R. H. Willett, W. M. Talbot, J. G. Warfield, E. F. Simpson, J. A. Ruff, Th. H. Langley, W. R. Hunt, Th. P. Morgan, Hy. T. Whalen, G. Th. Woodward, J. R. Riggles, W. H. Griffith, John Lanahan, G. G. Baker, B. Peyton Brown, T. H. Davis and J. Hy. Wilson, as incorporators.

It is a stock association, with the capital stock fixed at $20,000, divided into 1000 shares at $20 per share. One share entitles the owner to the privilege of a tent site, and five shares to a cottage site.

The land is held by a Board of Trustees, and its business is managed by an Executive Committee, who are elected annually.

Its general purposes are for holding Camp Meetings and building up summer homes for a select community.

Two surveys have been made, one for the tenting and the other for the cottage department; in the latter, the lots are 50 x 150 feet.

The tract consists of 268 acres, well wooded in white oak and chestnut timber, supplied with an abundance of the finest water in springs and wells, and some of it possessed of decided medicinal properties. It is considered as healthy a location as any in the State.

It is located on what is known as Parr's Ridge, a high point, over 600 feet above tide level, and on the line of the Metropolitan Railroad, 20½ miles from Washington, and in a north-east direction from Gaithersburg. The railroad passes through the edge of the tract, and a broad and shaded avenue leads direct from the railroad station to the camping grounds.

The first camp was held August 13th, 1873, and six camps have been held since to August, 1879. All the meetings were largely attended and satisfactory in results, more than four hundred and sixty-four persons having been converted at the different meetings.

The officers have been—

Dr. Flodoardo Howard.............*President.*
W. R. Woodward.................*Vice-President.*
E. F. Simpson....................*Secretary.*
J. A. Ruff.......................*Treasurer.*

The present officers are—

THOS. P. MORGAN.................*President.*
W. R. WOODWARD................*Vice-President.*
E. F. SIMPSON...................*Secretary.*
B. H. STINEMETZ.................*Treasurer.*

Rev. B. Peyton Brown, the present Presiding Elder of the Washington District, has been and is one of the leading spirits in this enterprise.

The Camping Grounds are laid out in an irregular seven sided "Circle," a plaza, from which as many avenues radiate, and all of these look direct into the plaza—which is 216 feet wide from North to South, and 179 feet from West to East. In the centre is a Tabernacle 48x70 feet, and the Camp is provided with a dining court and other necessary structures.

Attention having been attracted to the Cottage Tent, as a desirable form for camp purposes, a number have been built, mostly on the plaza—and are named in the order of their location. Rev. W. Burris, Thos. P. Morgan, E. F. Simpson, Alfred Wood, J. W. St. Clair, Henry C. Craig, Jr., L. W. Worthington, J. W. Wade, Thos. Somerville, Geo. E. Hall, John Ireland, (of Annapolis,) H. W. Frankland, W. R. Woodward, R. Cohen, Jr. and R. H. Willett; on Second Avenue, Mrs. Kilgore, of the

County; on Sixth Avenue, a Preachers' Lodge, and on Second Avenue extended a Keeper's house.

Messrs. Willett & Morgan were the pioneers in cottage building.

On First Avenue, Mr. Wash. B. Williams has a commodious furniture store and lodging house.

Other improvements are contemplated that will make Washington Grove a most desirable and attractive spot.

The organization is under the control of the Methodist Episcopal Church, but persons of all denominations unite with them, and are heartily welcome.

# DIRECTORY

OF THE

# TOWNS, VILLAGES AND RESIDENTS

OF

# MONTGOMERY COUNTY, MD.

## BARNESVILLE,

One mile from the Station by that name on the Metropolitan Branch, Baltimore and Ohio Railroad, 73 miles from Baltimore, and 33 miles from Washington. Soil—poor, but susceptible of great improvement. Products, per acre—15 bushels Wheat, 20 bushels Corn, 1500 ℔s. Tobacco, one ton Hay. Four Churches—Methodist, Roman Catholic, Baptist, and Protestant Episcopal. Population, 175.

*Postmaster.*

Pyles, R. T.

*Blacksmiths and Wheelwrights.*

Miles, C. W.
Miles, N, E.

*Carpenters and Undertakers.*

Hilton, W. T.
Orme, A. S.

*Merchants.*

Darby, S., & Sons.
Harris, E. G.
Hays, R. P.
Pyles, R. T.

*Hotels.*

Carr, W. H.
Talbot, N. J.

*Millers.*

Darby, John W.
Darby, R. R.

*Physicians.*

Bowlen, G. W.
Wood, R. Vinton.

*Shoemaker.*

Nichols, Charles S.

*Farmers.*

Bowman, Frederick
Cooley, J. F.
Cooley, Z. G.
Darby, J. W.
Harris, A. S.
Harris, S. F.
Hays, F. P.
Hays, L. J.
Hays, S. S.
Hershey, C. R.
Hodges, William
Lawman, Charles
Lawman, James
Linthicum, F.
Lynch, John H.
Pearre, Jamez
Poole, A.
Reid, W. N.
Sellman, L. L.
Sellman, J. P.
Sellman, Wm. O.
Wade, W. W.
Ward, Thomas H.
White, R. G.
White, W. B.

## BEALLSVILLE,

Three miles from Barnesville, on the Metropolitan Railroad, and three miles from Poolesville. Land under clean cultivation. Soil sandy, and producing good crops of Wheat, Corn, and Hay. Churches and Schools. Store, Post Office, Wheelwright and Blacksmith Shop. Population, 50.

*Farmers.*

Beall, L.
Brewer, W. G.
Bolinger, W.
Griffith, H.
Griffith, Frank

Griffith, P.
Hemstone, A. T.
Trail, Richard
Veirs, J. M.
Webster, George
Whiting, ———

## BETHESDA,

On the Frederick and Georgetown Pike, five miles from Georgetown, D. C., and three miles from Knowles' Station on the Metropolitan Railroad. Soil fertile, selling from thirty dollars to one hundred and twenty-five dollars per acre. Products—Wheat, 25 to 50 bushels, Corn, 45 bushels, Hay, two and one-half tons per acre. Presbyterian Church and Public School. Population, 25.

*Postmaster.*

Lester, R. C.

*Attorney at Law.*

Bradley, Joseph

*Blacksmiths.*

Kirby, Wm.
Loehte, Wm.

*Carpenter.*

Beckwith, Benedict

*Carriage Maker.*

Austin, James

*Merchandise.*

Lester, R. C.

*Physician.*

Davidson, James H.

*Farmers.*

Anderson, J. Hopkins
Bean, A. H. and B. F.
Bean, E. H. and Jas. M.
Bohrer, J. T. and John G.
Bradley, Joseph
Carroll, H. G.
Counselman, Wm.
Davidson, James H.
Davidson, John
Dodge, J. H.

Dunlap, George
Gingel, James M.
Gingel, Joseph
Gleghorn, John
Hudleston, Geo. and Wm.
Jones, L. C.
Keizer, Cyrus
Keizer, Eli
Kisner, C.
Kisner, Henry
Lawrence, David
Lester, R. C.
Offutt, H. L.
Owens, Z.
Powell, James
Pyles, Henry
Renshaw, Henry
Renshaw, Thomas
Renshaw, William
Spates, Frank
Spates, George
Spates, Robert
Tolbert, Theophilus
Wallis, Edwin
Watkins, E. P.
Watkins, Spencer
Williams, John C.
Williams, Lewis
Willson, John N.
Willson, Michael

## BOYD'S,

On the Metropolitan Branch, Baltimore and Ohio Railroad, seventy miles from Baltimore, and thirty miles from Washington, is one of the handsomest points on the Metropolitan Railroad, and is being rapidly improved. This is in a great measure due to Captain James A. Boyd and Messrs. Williams and Lewis. Captain Boyd has expended over one hundred thousand dollars in improvements in the past few years. Location very healthy, being five hundred feet above the level of the sea. Business, crops, and land good, with a clay soil, ranging in price from ten dollars to one hundred dollars per acre. Produces 15 to 35 bushels Wheat, 45 bushels Oats, 100 bushels Potatoes, 60 bushels Corn, and 1000 pounds of Tobacco to the acre. Liberal inducements and well improved lands; excellent water-power, suitable for extensive manufacturing purposes. Presbyterian Church, Rev. James S. Henderson, Pastor. White and Colored Public Schools. Population, 100.

*Postmaster.*
> Williams, James E.

*Blacksmith.*
> Howard, James

*Merchants.*
> Williams & Lewis.

*Millers.*
> Darby, John W. & Son.
> Davis, R. P.
> Waters, Dr. W.

*Dairies.*
> Boyd, James A.
> Burdette, Basil
> Burdette, R. H.

*Farmers.*
> Beall, J. H.
> Boyd, James A.
> Brewer, D. N.

Burdette, Basil
Burdette, R. H.
Burdette, Wm. M.
Carlin, John
Carlin, John T.
Dade, Alex.
Dade, Robert
Gott, Benj. C.
Grant, Robert N.
Knott, Frances
Knott, John W.
McAtee, James W.
McAtee, John S.
Thompson, Baker
White, Joseph C.
White, R. T.
Williams & Lewis.

*Pomologist.*
> Meigs, F. P.

## BRIGHTON,

Four miles East of Brookeville, near the Patuxent River, contains several Stores and Post Office, and is noted for the superior quality of Sweet Corn and Fruits. Land under fine tillage and very productive; rated at twenty to sixty dollars per acre. Population, 150.

*Merchants.*
> Pierce, E. & Co.

*Fruit Packer.*
> Stabler, Henry

*Insurance Agent.*
> Hartshorne, Isaac

9

## BROOKEVILLE

Is forty-two miles from Baltimore, eighteen miles from Washington, and ten miles from Rockville; pleasantly located in one of the richest sections of the County, and is quite a fashionable resort in the summer for health and pleasure seekers,—the restorative qualities of a strong Chalybeate Spring in the vicinity attracting many persons anxious to try its efficacy. The lands are highly improved and under thorough cultivation. Soil, red clay; selling from fifteen to one hundred dollars per acre. The productions are large and increasing; business good. Churches— Methodist Protestant, Methodist Episcopal, and the Protestant Episcopal Chapel. One Academy, Prof. Samuel H. Coleman, Principal. One Public School. Population, 250.

*Postmaster.*

Gattrell, R. W.

*Blacksmiths.*

Conner, James
Jones, Wm. H.
Kirby, Thomas

*Carpenter.*

Appleby, A. O.

*Carriages and Wagons.*

Baker, John M.
Boswell, R. K.
Miller, Wm. B.

*Merchants.*

Gattrell, R. W.
Mobley, Wm. B.
Parsley, John H.

*Harness.*

Bell, John W.

*Millers.*

Down, Wm. H.
Weir & Bro.

*Physicians.*

Martin, James S.
Riggs, Artemus

*Shoemakers.*

Parsley, George W.
Whiteside, John

*Seamstress.*

Parsley, Margaret

*Watchmaker.*

Howard, Henry N.

*Farmers.*

Clark, John O.
Davis, Hon. A. Bowie
Ellicott, Samuel
Gaither, Daniel H.
Gaither, Ephraim
Gaither, John W.
Gaither, Thos. D.
Gardiner, John W.
Gattrell, Aaron
Griffith, John
Hall, E. J.
Hallowell, James S.
Higgins, C. A. C.
Holland, James T.
Holland, Thos. J.
Howard, Mrs. Annie N.
Howard, Brice W.
Hutton, Joseph W.
Hutton, Rev. Orlando
Jones, G.
Magruder, Bowie
Owen, Hon. E. W.
Riggs, Thos. D.
Riggs, Wm. C.
Stabler, James
Strain, Capt. J. W.
Veitch, Fletcher R.
Waters, Thos. D.
Waters, Z. D.

## BURTONSVILLE,

Five and one half miles from Laurel.  Soil, arable, and principally cleared ; land sells from fifteen to sixty dollars per acre.  20 to 30 bushels Wheat, 25 to 50 Corn, and Hay, two tons per acre.  Liberty Grove Church, Pastor, Rev. J. Cook.  Population, 50.

*Postmaster.*
  Burton, R. A.
*Blacksmiths and Wheelwrights.*
  Beall, Joseph
  Burton, R. A.
  Robey, Berry
*Carpenters.*
  Beall, Joseph
  Homer, M. J.
  Mineburg, John
  Vincent, Plummer
*Merchant.*
  Small, Bruce
*Miller.*
  Bone, Allen
*Physician.*
  Waters, Charles
*Farmers.*
  Beall, John
  Beall, Josiah
  Beall, Nathan F.
  Beall, Thos.
  Bone, Allen

Burton, George D.
Burton, George H.
Burton, Isaac
Carr, A. B.
Carr, B. D.
Carr, Caleb
Crosedale, Howard
Crosedale, John
Crusen, Henry S.
Harding, Samuel H.
Hopkins, James H.
Iglehart, James L.
Iglehart, Nathan
Marshall, James
Miller, John
Rich, Charles
Rich, William
Soper, James P.
Soper, Joseph
Thomas, Samuel
Ward, Orem
Waters, Charles
Waters, J.
Waters, T., Sr.
Waters, T., of S.
Waters, T. J.

## CABIN JOHN

Is at the crossing of the Aqueduct over Cabin John Creek.  This crosses on a single arch, the longest span in the world.  A fashionable resort for pleasure parties from Washington; the fishing for Bass in the Potomac being excellent.  Hotel, Store and Post Office.

## CEDAR GROVE,

Five miles from Germantown.  Land variable.  Soil—clay, flint and rock ; worth from ten to thirty dollars per acre.  Wheat, 25 to 30 bushels ; Corn, 30 to 40; Tobacco, 1500 pounds, and Hay, one ton per acre.  Two Churches—Methodist Episcopal and Baptist.  White and Colored Schools in vicinity.  Population, 125.

*Postmaster.*

Watkins, O. T.

*Blacksmiths.*

Majors, John T.
Miles, George

*Carpenter.*

Waters, F. M.

*Merchandise.*

Watkins, O. T.

*Farmers.*

Appleby, Curtis
Barber, G. E.
Barber, H.
Beall, G. N.
Bowman, Asbury
Burns, Sylvester
Miles, Herbert

Page, Horace
Page, Washington
Page, Z. W.
Poole, W. H.
Pugh, Samuel
Purdum, J. R.
Riggs, James
Riggs, W. E.
Sibley, Joseph
Thompson, Wm.
Watkins, B. F.
Watkins, E. K.
Watkins, James W.
Watkins, L. L.
Watkins, Noah
Williams, J. F.
Williams, Somerset
Williams, Wm.
Young, Richard

# CLARKSBURG.

This picturesque village is located on the Washington and Frederick Turnpike, fifteen miles from Frederick, thirty miles from Washington, and four and one-half miles from Boyd's Station. The land in and around Clarksburg was originally granted to Henry Griffith in 1761, and known as the "Cow Pasture." The first house built in the village was by John G. Clark, whose daughter married William Wilson, the father of Leonidas Wilson, the present owner, who, for a long time, successfully conducted the business of merchandising. It is now occupied by Lewis & Williams. In the garden of Mr. Scholl, at the east end of the village, was first discovered the celebrated Catawba Grape, which has since gained such a world renowned reputation. It is now owned by the Hon. George W. Hilton, and is annually visited by numbers of Pomologists and curiosity seekers. Great improvement has been made in the land during the past few years by the aid of lime and fertilizers, and can be purchased from ten to sixty dollars per acre. Produces 20 to 30 bushels of Wheat, 30 to 50 of Corn, 35 of Oats, 100 of Potatoes, 1200 to 1500 pounds of Tobacco, and two tons of Hay per acre. Two Churches, both Methodist Episcopal. White and Colored Public Schools. Odd Fellows Hall. Literary Association. King's Distillery. Population, 250.

*Postmaster.*

Buxton, Wm. H.

*Blacksmiths and Wheelwrights.*

Anderson, C. T.
Dronenberg, Wm. W.
Leaman, R. A.
Shaw, L. D.

*Justice of the Peace.*

Belt, John S.

*Carpenters.*

Leaman, John S.
Woodward, C. O.

*Hotel.*

Baker, John

*Merchants.*

Gibson, John H.
Lewis & Williams.

*Physicians.*
Galloway, T. K.
Thompson, R. H.
Waters, Wm. A.
*Tax Collector.*
Neal, James B.
*Shoemaker.*
Hurley, John W.
*Publishers.*
Boyd, T. H. S. & Co.
*Mills.*
King, Luther G.
*Distillery.*
King, L. G.
*Tobacco Inspector.*
Hilton, Robert S.
*Tailor.*
Housen, Lewis
*Farmers.*
Beall, Caleb
Belt, John S.
Boyd, Elizabeth
Burns, J. W.
Darby, Edward N.
Darby, Nathan
Day, James W.

Dronenberg, Wm. J.
Hilton, Hon. George W.
Hoyle, Jos. H. C.
Johnson, James T.
Israel, George W.
Kemp, James S.
King, Charles M.
King, Edward J.
King, Rufus
Layton, O. S.
Lewis, Edward
Lewis, John A.
Linthicum, Gassaway W.
Miles, James H.
Murphey, C. R.
Neal, James B.
Purdum, Charles T.
Purdum, James H.
Rose, A.
Rose, S. L.
Summers, C.
Summers, Z.
Thompson, Samuel C.
Waters, A. J.
Waters, Edward H.
Waters, Dr. Wm. A.
Watkins, William, of A.
Williams, Wm.
Williams, Wm. L.
Windsor, Wm. R.

## COLESVILLE,

On the Ashton and Colesville Turnpike, eight miles from Silver Springs, and sixteen miles from Washington. Land under fair cultivation, and yielding good crops of Wheat, Corn, Oats, Potatoes, and Hay. Land worth from twenty-five to seventy-five dollars per acre. Churches, Schools, Mills, Stores, and Post Office.

*Magistrate.*
Baker, John T.
*Miller.*
Zeigler, James H.
*Butcher.*
Hopkins, Samuel J.
*Farmers.*
Baker, John T.

Bonifant, George
Bradley, W. P.
Canby, Wm. M.
Fawcett, E. H.
Fawcett, Benjamin
Hopkins, Samuel J.
Pilling, Frank A.
Valdenar, William
Walters, E. L.

## DAMASCUS,

Seven miles from Mount Airy, on the Baltimore and Ohio Railroad. General products—Wheat, Corn, Tobacco, and Hay. Land undulating, selling from eight to twenty-five dollars per acre. Montgomery Chapel, (Methodist Protestant,) and Howard Chapel, (Methodist Episcopal.) Schools near. Population, 100.

*Postmaster.*
> Smith, P. M., Jr.

*Blacksmith.*
> Smith, James W.

*Carpenters and Undertakers.*
> Edwards, Henry C.
> Mount, John R.

*Carriages and Wagons.*
> Jacobs, Jonathan
> Ward, N. H.

*Merchants.*
> Clagett, J. H.
> Engle, R.
> Etchison, Marcellus
> Hurley, R. A.
> Smith, P. M., Jr.
> Young & King.

*Harness.*
> Burns, R. R.

*Physician.*
> Lansdale, B. F.

*Shoemaker.*
> Holland, S. B.

*Farmers.*
> Bowman, Rezin H.
> Burdette, James W.
> Burdette, N. J.
> Burns, Jesse L.
> Day, Rev. Jackson
> Duvall, M.
> Duvall, R.
> Glaze, Bazil T.
> Gue, L. C.
> Hilton, Thomas I.
> Hilton, Walter
> King, C. M.
> Mullinix, George W.
> Purdum, C. F.
> Scheckles, J. T.
> Warfield, John
> Warfield, John E.
> Warthen, N. B.
> Watkins, Grafton
> Watkins, P. G.

## DARNESTOWN,

Five miles from Germantown Station, Metropolitan Railroad. Land productive, and plenty for sale at from fifteen to eighty dollars per acre. Produces abundant crops of Wheat, Corn, Oats, Potatoes, Tobacco, and Hay. Presbyterian Church, Academy, and Public School. Population, 200.

*Postmaster.*
> Windsor, J. S.

*Merchants.*
> Griffith, Julian
> Windsor, James S.

*Millers.*
> Darby, Upton
> Offutt, U. D.

*Farmers.*
> Beall, Randolph
> Benton, James N.
> Broon, Duthorn
> Cross, J.
> Dawson, Nicholas
> Higdon, John
> Higgins, Samuel
> Jones, Nathan

Lewis, Thomas
Magruder, Thomas
Purdum, James W.
Rice, William

Small, John
Thompson, Martin
Vincent, Barley
Vincent, Charles

## DAWSONVILLE,

Four and a half miles from Boyd's Station. Sandy soil, and land principally cleared and valued at from thirty to eighty dollars per acre. Produces large crops of Wheat, Corn, Oats, Potatoes, and Tobacco. A Baptist Church and Public School. Population, 75.

*Postmaster.*
Allnutt, H. C.
*Blacksmith.*
Stang, F. C.
*Merchandise.*
Allnutt, H. C.
*Physician.*
White, N. S.
*Shoemaker.*
Crown, Wm.
*Farmers.*
Allnutt, Benjamin
Allnutt, Berroni
Allnutt, James N.

Allnutt, Nathan W.
Byrd, John
Darby, Thomas
Dawson, Americus
Dawson, Fred. A.
Dawson, James M.
Dawson, Randolph
Dyson, Benjamin
Dyson, Joseph
Dyson, Samuel
Jones, Thomas
Pyles, B. Frank
Pyles, Edward
Rawlings, Joshua
Rawlings, Thomas
Vincent, Napoleon

## DICKERSON,

Thirty-six miles on the Metropolitan Branch, Baltimore and Ohio Railroad. Land well cleared and clay soil; valued at from thirty to fifty dollars per acre. Under good cultivation, and yielding 35 bushels of Wheat, 40 of Corn, 1000 pounds of Tobacco, and two tons of Hay to the acre. Churches and Schools in the immediate vicinity. Population, 100.

*Postmaster.*
Dickerson, W. H.
*Dairies.*
Bowie, Rufus A.
Holland, J. W.
*Merchants.*
Dickerson, W. H.
Leapley, J. N.
*Physician.*
Hilton, L. J. W.

*Millers.*
Rozzell, James
Webster, George
Willing, Ambrose.
*Farmers.*
Andrews, Jefferson
Appleby, N. H.
Belt, McGill
Belt, Richard
Brall, Wm.
Brall, Rufus

Carslisle, James
Carson, David
Cheswell, E.
Dickerson, N. C.
Diggins, Daniel
Gott, J. S.
Harris, Abraham
Harris, Solomon T.
Hays, G. R.
Heffener, John
Hempstone, A. T.
Hempstone, S. H.
Jones, J. A.
Jones, J. L. T.
Jones, J. T.
Jones, Leo
Luhn, Chris.
Moxley, Thomas
Moxley, Wm.

Oden, George W.
Price, John T.
Price, Wm.
Ramhouse, Sydney
Riely, Otho
Scholl, Henry
Sellman, F. O.
Sellman, Howard
Silence, John
Titus, Burr
Trundle, Horatio
Trundle, James O.
White, Frank
White, R. G.
White, L. A.
Whitehouse, M. O.
Yarkund, Hildi
Zerknitz, Hans

---

## EDWARDS' FERRY,

On the Potomac River, between Sycamore Landing and Ball's Bluffs, contains Store, Warehouse and Post Office.

*Postmaster.*
   Spates, George W.

*Farmers.*
   Collier, Thomas R.

Elgin, James
Jarboe, E. E.
Poole, N. D.
Spates, George W.
White, E. V.

---

## FAIRLAND,

Three miles East of Colesville, on the Columbia Road. St. Mark's Memorial Episcopal Church, School House and Store. Population, 50.

*Postmaster.*
   Soaper, Burton T.

*Farmers.*
   Barrett, Benjamin
   Beckwith, B.
   Beckwith, E.
   Brian, John M.
   Culver, J. H.

Conley, Thomas T.
Mankin, J. D.
Marlow, Benj. H.
Marlow, Julius
Mitchell, Daniel
Pilling, Alice
Roby, Edgar
Soaper, Joseph

## FOUR CORNERS,

Two miles from Silver Springs. Land productive and worth from twenty to fifty dollars per acre. Wheat, Corn, and Hay are the staple productions. Methodist Episcopal Church (South), and Public School. Population, 125.

*Postmaster.*

Grimes, Robert

*Blacksmith.*

Taylor, B.

*Carpenters.*

Berry, John
Chrismond, Robert
Reynolds, Gassaway

*Merchandise.*

Manakee, Wm. E.

*Millers.*

Bond, James H.
Bond, James L.

*Shoemakers.*

Grimes, Robert
Lancaster, John W.

*Farmers.*

Adams, C.
Barnes, Henry A.
Barnes, William
Bayley, Stephen
Beall, George N.
Boarman, Robert
Bowie, Henry
Cadle, William
Chrismond, Robert

Clark, Bailey
Clark, E.
Clark, Henry
Clark, James
Clark, Levin
Clark, Oliver
Clark, O. H. P.
Clark, William
Fee, William
Fee, William, Jr.
Gittings, William, Sr.
Grimes, William M.
Hardesty, Thomas G.
Hopkins, Joseph
Jackson, Jasper M.
Joy, Columbus
Lindsay, Opie H.
Mackmahon, Michael
Moran, Andrew
Ogdon, Leonard
Ogdon, Wm. J.
Olin, Hon. A. B.
Owings, James
Parker, James
Patten, L. P.
Reed, William
Shaw, Charles H.
Vermillion, John H.

## GAITHERSBURG,

Twenty-one miles from Washington, on the Metropolitan Branch, Baltimore and Ohio Railroad. This place was incorporated by the last Legislature and is rapidly improving. The land principally is in a fine state of cultivation, and is valued in price from fifteen to one hundred dollars per acre, and produces 40 to 50 bushels of Wheat, 60 of Corn, two tons of Hay, and 1500 pounds of Tobacco to the acre. Two Churches—Methodist Episcopal, South, and Roman Catholic. Town Hall and Public School. Population, 200.

*Postmaster.*

Ward, H. C.

*Agent Railroad.*

Poole, S.

*Blacksmiths.*

Duvall, C. F.
Easton, Giles
Gloyd, Samuel

*Carpenters.*

Beckwith, Greenbury
Beckwith, Waters

*Merchants.*

Belt, John H.
Owen, T. J.
Ward & Fulks.

*Millers.*

Lemon, George
Trail, Burton
Watkins, Levi

*Physician.*

Etchison, E. E.

*Shoemaker.*

Cooms, William

*Farmers.*

Briggs, Gideon
Briggs, James M. N.
Briggs, John
Briggs, Robert
Briggs, Samuel
Briggs, Thomas
Calvin, Timothy
Chandle, J. W.
Clagette, James H.
Clagette, John H.
Clements, Lemuel
Clopper, D.
Codwise, B. R.

Cook, Nathan
Cook, Wm. H.
Cooke, Mrs. E.
Cooke, Wm. J.
Crown, H. L.
Day, Jacob
Day, Washington
Dessellum, John T.
Diamond, J. B.
Diamond, Mrs. S. J.
Dorsey, R. G.
Fulks, Wm. R.
Gaither, James B.
Gaither, W. R.
Hutton, W. R.
Jones, L. C.
Meesne, C. G.
Meesne, O. C.
Mills, Richard
Reed, William
Ricketts, Isaac
Selby, Allen
Selby, John T.
Small, John
Suter, Thomas R.
Thompson, F. H.
Thompson, John
Thompson, Joseph
Tscheffely, F. H.
Wade, John W.
Wade, William
Walker, G. E.
Walker, J. W.
Walker, N. J.
Whalen, Martin
Woodward, R.

# GERMANTOWN,

Twenty-seven miles from Washington, on the Metropolitan Branch, Baltimore and Ohio Railroad. Good land and excellent water; valued at from ten to fifty dollars per acre. The soil is kind, yielding productively of Wheat, Corn, Oats, Potatoes, Tobacco, and Hay.

The village is located about one mile from the Station; contains two Churches—Methodist Episcopal and Baptist, and Public School. Quite an extensive business is carried on at the Station in Fertilizers and Agricultural Implements; also, in the Manufacture of Carriages, Buggies, &c. Population, 100.

*Postmaster.*

Thomas N. Henderson.

*Agent.*

Gassaway, John H.

*Harness, &c.*

Nicholls, John H.

*Merchants.*

Gassaway, John H.
Harris, R. E.
Henderson, Thomas N.
Waters, Horace D.

*Shoe and Boot Maker.*

Carlin, Thomas

*Farmers.*

Bennett, R. H.
Benson, John T.
Benson, Wm. H.

Gassaway, John H.
Gloyd, Eden
Henderson, Joseph
Laurer, J. A.
Leaman, Christian
Musser, William
Page, Nathan
Pumphreys, Henry
Reichter, John C.
Snyder, Jacob F.
Snyder, John
Waters, Horace
Waters, William
Williams, Henry
Williams, Samuel

## GOSHEN,

Five miles from Gaithersburg. Land in fine cultivation. Soil—clay, mixed with loam, and valued at from twenty to fifty dollars per acre. Produces 30 bushels of Wheat, 50 of Corn, 1000 pounds of Tobacco, and two tons of Hay per acre. One Church—Methodist Episcopal, South Public School, two Mills, &c. Population, 50.

*Postmaster.*

Martin, A. R.

*Blacksmith.*

Hogan, C. F.

*Merchandise.*

Martin, A. R.

*Millers.*

Davis, J. S.
Lewis, J. W.

*Farmers.*

Benson, J. E.
Blunt, W. W.
Bowman, Uriah G.
Dorsey, R. G.
Green, Richard
Higgins, James
Higgins, Thomas
Jones, Richard W.

Jones, Somerset O.
La Mar, J. C.
Magruder, H. R.
Magruder, J. S.
Magruder, Wm. M.
Magruder, Z. M.
McMahan, E.
Merriweather, A. G.
Miller, Washington
Reed, William
Riggs, George
Riggs, Harry
Riggs, R. D.
Stewart, A. G.
Thompson, J. H.
Thompson, J. C.
Thompson, Wm., of C.
Waters, J. McC.
Waters, W. D.

## GREAT FALLS,

On the Potomac River. The Government Dam and Water Works are located here for supplying the District of Columbia. This is the largest available water-power in the world, and its development and utilization for manufacturing purposes, cannot fail to eventuate in the growth of a considerable town at this point.

The Great Falls Ice Companies' Warehouses are also located here. Hotel, Store and Post Office. Population, 150.

## HYATTSTOWN.

Eight miles from Boyd's, on Bennett's Creek. Soil—clay, mixed with slate. Land undulating, back to the foot of Sugar Loaf Mountain; is principally cleared and under good cultivation, and worth from eight to fifty dollars per acre. Producing of Wheat, 25 bushels; Corn, 50; Oats, 40; Potatoes, 100; Tobacco, 1000 pounds, and Hay, two tons per acre. Three Churches—Methodist Episcopal and Methodist Episcopal, South, and Christian. White and Colored Public Schools. Population, 150.

*Postmaster.*

Smith, J. R.

*Blacksmiths.*

Dutrow, Jacob W.
Dutrow, O. W.

*Carpenters and Undertakers.*

Dutrow, P. C.
Gardner & Son.
Smith, J. R.

*Carriages and Buggies.*

Brengle, J. H.

*Merchants.*

Dutrow, D. W.
Welsh, Wellington

*Miller.*

Darby, George A.

*Physician.*

Zeigler, A. H.

*Saddles and Harness.*

Burdett, John E.

*Shoemaker.*

Grimes, George

*Tailor.*

Davis, William

*Farmers.*

Anderson, Mrs. Ellen

Browning, Charles T.
Cecil, Otho F.
Dixon, John
Harris, Z. G.
Johnson, Samuel
Keith, C.
Lawson, James W.
Layton, C. F. & Bro.
Leather, E.
Lewis, J. R.
Lewis, William B.
McLane, Amon
McLane, Joshua
Price, Charles
Price, George
Price, Levi
Price, Thomas, of E.
Price, Thomas H.
Simmons, Samuel T.
Tabler, Andrew J.
Tabler, George F.
Tabler, J. L.
Tabler, John H.
Warfield, H. G.
Watkins, Luther
Welsh, Asa H.
Windsor, Z. L.
Wolfe, Jesse H.
Zeigler, D.

## HUNTING HILL,

Five miles West of Rockville, on the Poolesville road, and three miles South of Gaithersburg. Land improving, and yielding fair crops of Wheat, Corn, Potatoes, and Hay. An important feature is the Chrome

Pits in the vicinity. Store, Wheelwright and Blacksmith Shop, and Post Office.

## KNOWLES',

Eleven miles from Washington, on the Metropolitan Branch, Baltimore and Ohio Railroad. Land variable; valued at from forty to eighty dollars per acre. Yielding 30 to 40 bushels of Wheat, 50 to 60 of Corn, and two tons of Hay. Churches and Schools in immediate vicinity. Population, 75.

*Postmaster.*
  Corrick, Joshua
*Blacksmith.*
  Mulican, George
*Bricklayers and Plasterers.*
  Lincoln, William
  Rhoe, William
*Carpenters.*
  Blackwith, W. T.
  Blake, George
  Duvall, George
  Welch, Patrick
*Merchandise.*
  Fawcett, F. M.

*Farmers.*
  Baker, Nelson
  Brown, D. W.
  Brown, M. J.
  Clemens, John
  Duvall, Charles
  Duvall, James
  Hiffiner, John
  Knowles, George
  Manakee, William
  McDermott, John
  McDermott, Patrick
  Mulican, R.
  Perry, Humphrey
  Wilson, George

## LAYTONSVILLE,

Seven miles from Gaithersburg. Land under fair cultivation; mostly cleared, and rated at from ten to fifty dollars per acre. Produces 30 bushels of Wheat, 25 to 40 of Oats, 150 of Potatoes, 50 to 100 of Corn, 1200 pounds of Tobacco per acre. One Church—Methodist Episcopal. Two Public Schools. Population, 100.

*Postmaster.*
  Bell, F. L.
*Blacksmiths and Wheelwrights.*
  Gittings, John T.
  Parsley, Thomas
  Wicks & Kimble.
*Carpenters and Undertakers.*
  Easton, S. H.
  Houck, E. H.
*Harness Maker.*
  Myers, E. F.
*Merchants.*
  Kenny, W. H. H.
  Mobley, George W.

*Physician.*
  Crawford, B. B.
*Shoemaker.*
  Snyder, J. P.
*Tailor.*
  Sellman, John A.
*Farmers.*
  Allnutt, J. B.
  Allnutt, John
  Allnutt, John T.
  Allnutt, William
  Ayton, E. B.
  Bell, F. L.
  Bell, James T.

Bell, Silence
Bowman, George W.
Brown, Edward
Clagett, James W.
Clagett, Mrs. M. A.
Crawford, C. A.
Darby, W. A.
Dorsey, Thomas W.
Fish, Benjamin R.
Gattrel, G.
Griffith, C. H.
Griffith, U.
Griffith, U. H.
Griffith, Wm. R.
Hawkins, Wm.
King, S.
Nelson, O.

Plummer, Richard
Plummer, Robert
Pope, C. A.
Pope, James M.
Pugh, David L.
Ray, Nicholas
Riggs, Reuben
Riggs, Samuel, of G.
Riggs, Samuel, of S.
Stewart, Albert
Thompson, T.
Ward, J.
Warfield, J. G.
Warfield, John T.
Waters, George T.
Watkins & Clagett.
Williams, James

## MARTINSBURG,

Eight miles from Barnesville, on the road (two miles) from White's Ferry, on the Potomac River. Land fertile, with a good clay soil; generally cleared, and commands from twenty to fifty dollars per acre. Yielding fine crops of Wheat, Corn, Oats, and Hay. Churches and Public Schools convenient. Population, 75.

*Postmaster.*
   Reed, James W.
*Blacksmiths.*
   McKenzie, T.
   Peters, John
*Merchants.*
   Phillips Brothers.
   Reed & Trundle.
*Millers.*
   Devilbiss, J. A.
   Weller, Frank
*Shoemaker.*
   Thomas, C. W.
*Farmers.*
   Boteler, A. J.

Cowley, R. T.
Hickman, James B.
Jones, William T.
Jones, John L. T.
Mercer, W. E.
Mosburg, George
Mosburg, P. K.
Oxley, Edgar F.
Oxley, Thomas
Pool, B. R,
Reed, John
Remsburg, D. F.
Remsburg, William
Skinner, James
Smoot, R. W.
Stallings, Richard
Stephenson, John
Veirs, William F.

## MIDDLEBROOK,

Two miles West of the intersection of the Frederick Turnpike and Big Seneca, nine miles West of Rockville, and four miles East of Clarksburg. Land, medium; can be purchased at from ten to twenty dollars per acre. Yielding fine crops of Wheat, Corn, Oats, Hay, Potatoes, and Tobacco. Churches and Schools near. Population, 30.

*Postmaster.*

Clements, George H.

*Blacksmith.*

Smith, Peter

*Carpenters.*

Easton, William
Trail, Thomas

*General Merchandise.*

Clements, George H.

*Millers.*

Buxton, Leonard
Watkins, L. L.

*Farmers.*

Benson, J. N,
Benson, Johnson
Benson, Thomas E.
Case, John
Case, Zadoc
Crawford, H.
Gloyd, James A.
Rabbitt, James O.
Ray, D. A.
Ricketts, A. P.
Trail, James O.
Trail, R.
Ward, T. G.
Ward, W. E.

## MONOCACY,

On the Monocacy River, near the crossing of the Metropolitan Railroad.
Land productive, and ranging from ten to twenty dollars per acre.   Pro-
ducing good crops of Wheat and Corn.   Mills, Churches, and Public
Schools convenient.   Population, 20.

*Postmaster.*

Sellman, Frederick

*General Merchandise.*

Sellman, Frederick

*Physician.*

Hellen, ——

*Farmers.*

Bouic, Rufus A.
Beall, William A.
Hays, George R.
Sellman, Frederick

## MONTROSE,

Is one-half mile from Randolph.   The soil, red clay; valued at fifty to
sixty dollars per acre.   Yielding 25 bushels of Wheat, 80 of Corn, and
two tons of Hay.   Population, 100.

*Postmaster.*

Heley, Francis

*Blacksmith.*

Flach, Joseph

*Carpenter.*

Cramer, C.

*General Merchandise.*

Heley, Francis
Holmes, T.
Magruder, W. F.

*Miller.*

Orndorf, William

*Farmers.*

Bagley, H.
Baker, E.
Ball, Frank
Codwise, B. R.
Curtin, T.
Duffy, Peter
Halpin, C.
Hance, W.

Lyddam, T.
Magruder, S. W.
Magruder, William
Magruder, W. S.
Ricketts, E.

Veirs, C.
Veirs, E.
Wilson, O.
Windan, George

# NORBECK

Is situated five miles from Rockville. The land is valued at twenty-five to forty dollars per acre. Yielding from 25 to 30 bushels of Wheat, 20 to 25 of Corn, and one and a half ton of Hay. Churches and Schools in close proximity. Population, 40.

*Postmaster.*
Bennett, John A.
*Blacksmith.*
Gill, James
*Carriage Maker.*
Cashell, C. R.
*General Merchandise.*
Bennett, John A.
Flack, A. C.
Ramier, James
*Carpenters.*
Burris, William
Nicholls, Charles

*Farmers.*
Abert, Charles
Abert, Robert W.
Adamson, R. L.
Beall, J. W.
Brooke, Albin
Brooke, Roger
Cashell, Thomas
Cashell, William
Flack, A. C.
Muncaster, Wm. E.
Nicholls, C. W.
Riley, P. C.
Sullivan, Perry
Thompson, William

# OFFUTT'S ✛ ROADS,

Six miles from Rockville, and two and a half miles from the Great Falls of the Potomac, which is considered one of the greatest water-powers in the country. The land surrounding is fair, and contains gold mines, which are now being worked. Land sells at from ten to thirty dollars per acre. Produces 15 to 30 bushels of Wheat, 100 of Potatoes, 25 of Oats, and 20 to 30 of Corn. Presbyterian and Methodist Episcopal Churches. Three Schools near. Population, 125.

*Postmaster.*
Offutt, William
*Blacksmiths.*
Lynch, William T.
McCormick, George
*Carpenters.*
Dolbeck, James
Hill, Lloyd
Sheppard, Thomas

*General Merchandise.*
Garrett & Maus.
McQuade, M.
Offutt & Perry.
*Gold Miners.*
Jas. Bartlett, Merritt & Co.
*Millers.*
McCormick, G.
Orendorf, Wm.
Storm, Philip & John

*Physicians.*
Offutt, B.
Willett, C. F.

*Shoemakers.*
Burriss, Lem. P.
Stearn, J. J.

*Farmers.*
Austin, Mahlon
Barnhouse, Richard
Boswell, Frank
Bradley, George G.
Bradley, Henry
Bradley, Henry, Jr.
Burriss, G. W.
Carroll, J. M.

Clagett, Darius
Clagett, Henry
Clagett, J. N.
Clagett, Wm.
Connell, John
Connell, Robert
Hardesty, Wm. M.
Hill, Levi
Kilgour, Frank
Maus, O. S.
Moore, J. D. W.
Offutt, John
Offutt, L. M.
Saunders, John
Stearn, Joseph
Trundle, John

# OLNEY

Is situated eight miles from Rockville. Land good, principally cleared; is valued at forty dollars per acre, and yields 25 bushels of Wheat, 50 of Corn, and 1200 pounds of Tobacco. Churches and Schools convenient. Population, 75.

*Postmaster.*
Kirk, R. L.

*Blacksmiths and Wheelwrights.*
Jones, L. D.
Walker, J. W.

*Carpenters and Undertakers.*
Groome, Thomas C.
Price, John
Young, R. W.

*Dairy.*
Farquhar, Greenville

*Dentist.*
Manakee, F. H.

*Merchandise.*
Barnesley, J. D.
Williams & Berger.

*Miller.*
Routzhan, M. C.

*Physician.*
Magruder, Wm. E.

*Shoemaker.*
Johnson, H. C.

*Stoves and Tinware.*
Wagner, J. L.

*Tailor.*
Schmitt, Andrew

*Farmers.*
Barnesley, George
Barnesley, James
Barnesley, Samuel
Berry, J. D.
Bowie, Col. W.
Brooke, C. F.
Cashell, G. C.
Cashell, H. B.
Cashell, S. S.
Chichester, W. B.
Childs, James O.
Childs, William
Dorsey, Col. G.
Duly, H. B.
Farquhar, Charles
Griffith, Thomas
Hallowell, H. C.
Higgins, H. O.
Holland, J. C.
Hyatt, George W.
Jones, L. W.
Kirk, Charles
Mackall, R. L.
Mackall, R. M.
Manakee, Reuben

10

## POOLESVILLE

Is located in the Horseshoe formed by the Potomac River, six miles from Barnesville Station, Metropolitan Railroad, and same distance from the Canal, and thirty-two miles from Washington. Principal products— Wheat, Corn and Hay. From fifteen hundred to two thousand head of Cattle are grazed for market in the District. Soil sandy, gray and red; ranging from fifteen to fifty dollars per acre. A Public and Private School largely attended; also, Briarly Hall Seminary for Young Ladies, ably conducted by Mrs. Mary E. Porter and daughter, with a large attendance. Population, 275.

*Postmaster.*

Cator, Samuel

*Blacksmith.*

Reed, Lewis

*Carpenters.*

Norris, William
Hall, E.
Money, J. H.

*Carriage Manufacturers.*

Straub & Son.

*Dentist.*

Schaeffer, Dr. T. H.

*Merchants.*

Hall, T. R.
Hays, William N.
Hoskinson Bros.
Kohlhoss, C.
Norris, J. T.

*Millers.*

Milford, Thos., & Bitzer.

*Physicians.*

Ayler, ——
Walling, ——
Wootton, ——

*Shoemakers.*

Grimes, Charles
Price, Elias

*Veterinary Surgeon.*

Poole, W. T. H.

*Farmers.*

Brewer, George
Brewer, William
Cecil, Humphrey
Cecil, William
Chiswell, Captain
Chiswell, Edward

Dade, John
Dawson, F.
Fisher, George
Fisher, Martin
Gott, Thomas N.
Griffith, Howard
Heirberger, Aaron
Hempstone, H. T.
Hempstone, T.
Hillard, Robert
Hughes, William D.
Jones, John A.
Jones, John L. T.
Jones, N.
Jones, William T.
Metzger, Charles
Metzger, William
Miles, Uriah
Poole, Dickerson
Poole, F. S.
Poole, J. Sprigg
Poole, Richard
Poole, Thomas H.
Poole, Wallace
Poole, William
Schaffer, William
Sellman, Charles
Talbott, Benson
Trundle, James
White, Benjamin
White, Frank
White, Joseph
White, Richard
White, Thomas H.
Willard, Charles
Willard, J.
Young, David
Young, Henry
Young, Isaac
Young, W. T.

## REDLAND,

Two miles from Derwood Station, Metropolitan Branch Railroad. Soil productive, and susceptible of improvement. Church and Public School. Population, 50.

*Postmaster.*

Peirce, H. B.

*Blacksmiths.*

Bready, C. W.
Bready, S. K.

*Carpenters.*

Belt, Rufus
Belt, W. M.

*Merchants.*

Peirce, H. B.
Thompson, H. S. & Bro.

*Miller.*

Shaw, Nathan

*Physicians.*

Magruder, J. W.
Magruder, Julian

*Farmers.*

Bean, C. M.
Bowman, U.
Case, J. & R.
Cashell, H.
Cashell, J.
Cashell, Thomas, Jr.
Griffith, David
Housholder, W. O.
Magruder, H. B.
Magruder, Zadoc
Muncaster, E. M.
Rabbitt, J.
Ricketts, J. T.
Riggs, Mrs. E. H.
Thompson, J. E.

## ROCKVILLE,

The County Seat, on the Metropolitan Railroad, fifty-seven miles from Baltimore, and sixteen miles from Washington. The land in the vicinity is clay loam, well improved, and sells from twenty to one hundred dollars per acre. Staple productions—Wheat, Corn, Hay, and Oats. Considerable attention is devoted to Fruit and Garden productions. Contains Court House, Jail, and the County Almshouse. Churches—Methodist Episcopal, Baptist, Presbyterian, Catholic, Episcopal, Disciples, and two Colored. Mispah Lodge, No. 144, A. F. & A. M. Montgomery Grange. Population, 1000.

*Postmaster.*

England, John G.

*Agents—Insurance.*

Higgins, John J.
Prettyman, E. D.

*Agent—Railroad.*

Cooper, J. J.

*Attorneys at Law.*

Anderson & Bouic.
Anderson, James W.
Brewer & Brewer.
Dawson, James

England, John G.
Jones, Spencer C.
Peter & Henderson.
Peter, John F.
Talbott, H. W.

*Auctioneer.*

Boswell, James

*Blacksmiths and Wheelwrights.*

Bagley, R. A.
Buxton, James F.
Green, M.
Haney, B.

Moulden, Eli
Mulfinger, J. P.

*Carpenters and Undertakers.*

Cator, George F.
Edmondson, John
Haney, Joseph
Pumphrey, W. R.

*Dentist.*

Manakee, F. H.

*Druggist.*

Owens, D. F.

*Harness Maker.*

Kircher, David

*Hotels.*

Montgomery—M. A. Almony.
Union—Francis Kleindienst.

*Livery Stables.*

Poss, J.
Rabbitt, W. H.

*Mason.*

Dwyer, Henry

*Merchants.*

Biays, J. P.
Bouic, D. H.
England, John G., Jr.
Higgins, S. D. & Son.
Lyddane, S. B.
Mulfinger, Mrs. Mary M.
Offutt, N. D.
Shekell, R. A.

*Millers.*

Veirs, E. & Brother.

*Millinery.*

Campbell, Misses
Cator, Mrs. G. F.
Miller, Mrs. J. R.

*Physicians.*

Maddox, C. J.
Sommers, A. A.
Stonestreet, E. E.

*Shoemakers.*

Johnson, R. R.
Sadtler, Louis
Steele, J. A.

*Tailor.*

Morgan, M.

*Tinner.*

Viett, Henry

*Watches and Jewelry.*

Ansley, Henry

*Wines and Liquors.*

Mullican, S. T.
Rabbitt, J. R.
Rabbitt, William H.

*Farmers.*

Anderson, Col. James
Anderson, James W., Jr.
Bedle, Amos
Belt, Edward C.
Bouic, Hon. W. V.
Bowie, Hon. R. I.
Brewer, John B.
Brooke, W. S.
Carter, R. W.
Claggett, Z. T.
Cromack, J. C.
Davis, Samuel L.
Dawson, H. A.
Dawson, John L.
Dove, Thomas R.
Edmondson, C. O.
Farquhar, Rodger B.
Gaither, William R.
Graff, George M.
Haney, Joseph M.
Higgins, James W.
Higgins, Mrs. S. D.
Horner, Frank B.
Horner, John W.
Hunter, Mrs.
Hunter, William
Hurley, Henry
Jones, William, Jr.
Keys, Chandler
Lyddane, S. M.
Maddox, Dr. Charles J.
Nelson, C. S.
Offutt, N. D.
Orndorff, W. O.
Prettyman, E. B.
Ray, N. K.
Ricketts, John H.
Ricketts, R. E.
Rozier, F. W.
Selby, Allen
Shaw, George
Shaw, James L.
Stonestreet, Dr. E. E.
Stonestreet, Samuel T.
Stonestreet, T. W.
Trail, Hezekiah
Veirs, E. M.

Veirs, W. A.
Wagner, J. N.
Watkins, Rudolph

White, George
Willson, John E.
Willson, Samuel

# SANDY SPRINGS,

Eight miles East of Rockville, and eleven miles from Laurel, is situated in the midst of a Settlement of Friends, and is surrounded by one of the wealthiest sections in the County. Land under a high state of cultivation, and improved by handsome buildings, etc. Land worth from twenty to one hundred dollars per acre. Principal productions—Wheat, Corn, Hay, and Fruit. Four Methodist Episcopal Churches, two Colored, and Society of Friends. Public and Private Schools. Mutual Fire Insurance Company, of Montgomery County; Sandy Springs Savings Bank, and Circulating Library. Population, 100.

*Postmaster.*

Stabler, Edward

*Blacksmiths.*

Budd, Samuel
Budd, Thomas
Marlow, J. F.
Turner, Fletcher

*Carpenters.*

Hill, Remus
Leizer, Francis
Moore, Robert S.
Tucker, Richard

*Merchants.*

Gilpin & Bentley.
Holland, James M.
Thomas, A. G.

*Millers.*

Brooke, Charles F.
Lea, Henry T.
White, Moab

*Physician.*

Iddings, C. Edward

*Farmers.*

Bready, John
Brooke, Alban
Brooke, George E.
Cashell, A. Jackson
Chandlee, Albert

Farquhar, William H.
Hallowell, Henry C.
Kirk, Mahlon
Lea, Edward
Lea, William
Miller, B. H,
Miller, Henry H.
Miller, Robert H.
Moore, Joseph T.
Moore, William W.
Palmer, B. D.
Palmer, P.
Roberts, B. R.
Scofield, William J.
Scott, Edmund
Smith, John M.
Stabler, Arthur
Stabler, Asa M.
Stabler, Charles
Stabler, Frederick
Stabler, Granville
Stabler, James P.
Stabler, Joseph
Stabler, Philip T.
Stabler, Robert M.
Stone, James H.
Thomas, Edward P.
Thomas, Francis
Thomas, Samuel P.
Thomas, William J.
Wetherald, Joseph

## SELLMAN'S,

On the Metropolitan Railroad, four miles West of Boyd's, and nine miles East of Point of Rocks, and one mile from Barnesville,—for which this is the Railway Station. *Railroad Agent,* Samuel Darby.

## SENECA,

On Great Seneca Creek, near its confluence with the Potomac River, on the road from Georgetown to Edwards' Ferry. Public Schools and Churches in the vicinity, Store and Post Office. *Postmaster,* Upton Dorsey.

## SLIGO,

One mile from Silver Springs, and six miles from Washington. Soil— light and loamy; land principally cleared, and rated at fifty to one hundred dollars per acre. Produces 30 bushels of Wheat, 25 of Corn, and two tons of Hay per acre. Methodist Protestant Church and two Catholic Churches. Two Public Schools. Population, 50.

*Postmaster.*
 Dorsey, James L.
*Blacksmiths.*
 Cunningham, C.
 Gentner, John
*Carpenter.*
 Long, J. D.
*Miller.*
 Bond, J. L.
*Physicians.*
 Harding, Josiah
 Stone, C. G.

*Farmers.*
 Blair, Hon. Montgomery
 Burch, R. W.
 Clark, O. H. P.
 Dorsey, James L.
 Draine, A. L.
 Fenwick, James
 Lee, S. P.
 Thompson, William
 Wilson, John C.
 Wilson, R. T.

## SPENCERVILLE,

On the road to Sandy Springs, and six miles from Burtonsville. Land productive, and yielding excellent crops of Wheat, Corn and Hay. Land worth from thirty to eighty dollars per acre. Baptist Church and Schools. Population, 100.

*Postmaster.*
 Spencer, W. H.
*Carpenter.*
 Barnes, James

*Nurseryman.*
 Phair, William H.
*Farmers.*
 Chaney, H. S.

Duvall, Louis H.
Herding, Joseph
Miller, W. P.
Reigle, George

Stabler, Asa M.
Stabler, Caleb
Stabler, F.

## SUNSHINE,

Ten miles from Gaithersburg. Soil good, and susceptible of improvement; can be bought from twenty to forty dollars per acre. Produces 25 bushels of Wheat, 40 of Corn, and two tons of Hay. Methodist Protestant, (Mount Carmel,) and Methodist Episcopal, (Unity Chapel.) Public School. Population, 150.

*Postmaster.*
Brown, William W.

*Blacksmiths.*
Davis, Nimrod
Grady, Frank

*Carpenters.*
Boswell, Nicholas
Brown, Franklin
Cashell, George

*Dentist.*
Dwyer, J. D.

*Merchants.*
Colliflower & Harvey.
Gaither, F. D.
Townsend, C. F.

*Machinist.*
Bozzell, J. Q.

*Physician.*
Maynard, J. H.

*Shoemakers.*
Brown, Uriah
Coomes, R. W.
Dwyer, J. W.

*Farmers.*
Brown, J. H.
Brown, Joshua
Brown, Robert
Curtis, John
Griffith, Frank
Groomes, Franklin
Hutton, C. C.
Kinsey, John G.
Lansdale, R. H.
Magruder, J. F. D.
Riggs, Elisha
Townsend, James
Watkins, O. P.

## TRIADELPHIA,

On the Patuxent River, north-east corner of Mechanicsville District. Soil productive. Products—30 bushels of Wheat, 40 of Corn, and 30 of Oats. Land from fifteen to sixty dollars per acre. Churches, Schools and Mills. *Postmaster,* Thomas Lansdale.

## WHEATON,

Half mile from Forest Glen. Location healthy. Soil—clay; land cleared, and rated at forty to eighty dollars per acre. Methodist Episcopal and Methodist Protestant Churches. Public School.

*Postmaster.*

Plyer, George

*Blacksmith.*

Rhine, A.

*Merchants.*

Anderson, D. C.
Davis, Charles
Jones, Samuel
Mitchell, Richard
Plyer, George
Ray, A.

*Physician.*

Harding, J.

*Farmers.*

Adams, Charles
Anderson, Charles
Batchelor, W. A.
Boher, Julius
Bowie, Allen
Bowman, William
Breaton, W.
Brown, Thomas
Burgdorf, A.
Childs, Joseph
Cropley, William
Dodge, J. P.

Dodge, Owen
Eccleston, Matthew
Federline, Frank
Glasgoe, J. E.
Hardy, Frank
Hardy, John
Haviland, James
Hunter, Thomas
Johnson, Henry
Jones, C. P.
Laney, John
Linkins, Henry
Matthews, Wesley
Muss, Peter
Noland, Thomas
Perry, Humphrey
Price, James
Price, William
Ray, Richard
Riley, Thomas
Stanton, Frederick
Stubbs, J. B.
Trucks, J.
Wallace, Murray
Weller, M.
Weller, William
Windham, A. J.

# WHITE'S FERRY,

Six miles from Poolesville, on the Potomac River, four miles from Leesburg, Virginia. Land in good cultivation; producing 30 to 40 bushels of Wheat; Corn, Oats, and Hay in proportion. Selling from thirty to seventy-five dollars per acre. Store and Post Office, with Churches and Schools in the neighborhood. Splendid Bass Fishing in the Potomac.

# PROMINENT MERCANTILE FIRMS

OF

# GEORGETOWN, D. C.

## THE LUMBER TRADE.

### WHEATLEY BROTHERS.

The City of Georgetown enjoys many advantages over other places favorable to the successful prosecution of the Lumber Trade, among which may be mentioned her central location and unsurpassed water facilities for receiving and shipping.

The immense amount of Lumber used annually in the United States is constantly increasing, and to supply this growing demand, an immense amount of capital and labor is invested. One of the oldest established firms so engaged in the District of Columbia is that of the Messrs. WHEATLEY BROTHERS, whose extensive yards in Georgetown and Washington cover fully four acres of ground. Some idea of the extent of their business may be inferred from the fact that they handle over seven million feet of Lumber yearly.

The Georgetown office is located at 37 *Water Street*, and the yards covering several acres are located on the *Banks of the Potomac and Rock Creek*, where they have a wharfage of three hundred feet, enabling vessels of any draught to load and unload at all times. Their stock embraces every description of Lumber received from all the different Lumber sections of the country.

At *Seventh Street and Rhode Island Avenue, in Washington*, their yard occupies one and one-half squares, and is connected with the Georgetown office by a Telephone, making communication easy and facilitating business.

In 1845, Mr. F. Wheatley, the father of the gentlemen conducting the present business established himself in Georgetown, and by his energy and enterprise, successfully conducted the business until 1866, when his four sons under the above style and name became proprietors, and since that time have illustrated the fact that the mantle of the sire fell on worthy shoulders, for they have materially extended and enlarged the business, keeping pace with the modern development of trade and commerce. Directing their entire time and energy, coupled with their extensive experience, exclusively to their business, and losing no opportunity of protecting their customers, it is certain that the "Brothers Wheatley" will merit a continuance of the generous support so long extended to them during the past.

The firm are enabled to transact business in a manner satisfactory to all concerned, and their prices are such that they can compete with Baltimore or more Eastern markets. Their trade is principally local, although they make shipments by the railroads and canal to Montgomery and adjacent Counties in Maryland and Virginia.

They are also largely engaged in building. Mr. Samuel E. Wheatley, one of the senior members of the Washington branch having immediate supervision of that department. They have twenty-six handsome brick dwellings on the square bounded by Seventh, Sixth and Q Streets and Rhode Island Avenue, and a number in the immediate neighborhood, all of which are occupied. They are all finished in modern style, combining all the conveniences for house-keeping.

Mr. Charles Wheatley, who has charge of the Georgetown office, is a social and genial gentleman—qualities, when joined with strict business principles, and honorable and upright dealing, is sure to make him a host of friends.

## GROCERIES, WHOLESALE AND RETAIL.

### S. CROPLEY'S SONS.

Among the important commercial enterprises of Georgetown which commend themselves to general notice, no one possesses features of greater interest than that of the Wholesale and Retail Grocery Trade. The house of S. CROPLEY'S SONS was established by Mr. Samuel Cropley in 1828, and succeeded by his two sons R. B. and A. B. Cropley in 1868, by whom it has since been prosecuted with great success. The individual importance of this house is such that it exerts an influence over the commercial interests of Georgetown, which is strongly felt by dealers in other departments of trade.

In addition to their Grocery Department, they are largely engaged in Rectifying Spirits and Compounding Liquors, among which they make a specialty of "*Old Club*" Whiskeys, of which they are sole proprietors; also of "Cropley's" X, XX, XXX Whiskeys.

They occupy a large five story building *Corner Bridge Street and Market Space*, where their wholesale business is principally carried on, and one at the *Corner of Bridge and Congress Streets*, which is devoted to supplying families with Fine Wines, Groceries and Canned Goods and Fruits, etc.

They are also extensive dealers in Tobacco, Snuff, Cigars, etc., of which they keep a well assorted stock, which is of great convenience and value to country dealers.

The Messrs. Cropley are Agents for Hazard's Powder, the celebrity of which is wide-spread. They make a specialty of this article, which is extensively used in every section of the country. As the attention of dealers to this house may be advantageous both to it and to themselves, these gentlemen, as agents, are prepared to supply it in any quantities, and at prices lower than it can be bought in the general market.

Their trade in Groceries is large, local and general through the District and the States adjoining. These goods are, strictly speaking, first-class when so represented, the high commercial standing of the house forbidding their imposition of goods upon customers of a quality inferior to the class ordered, for the temporary emolument such a transaction might afford. In every respect the house of S. Cropley's Sons is a good one, meriting universal patronage.

---

## AN ENTERPRISING MAN.

### ROBERT T. ARLOW.

It has always been the boast of the American citizen that no country in the world offers better opportunlties for the truly enterprising, or where true worth will quicker bring a reward than in the United States. An instance of the truth of this statment appears in the case of Mr. ROBERT T. ARLOW, 82 *Water Street, Georgetown*. This well known, energetic and successful business man is an example where industry and careful management have led to unqualified success. Mr. Arlow started business here in the year 1865, his cash capital being only five dollars. Being ambitious, prudent and withal determined to succeed, he kept constantly increasing his business and using all possible means to advance his interests, and to-day he is the owner of considerable property. His active and energetic manner of doing business, combined with his genial and pleasant manners, has made him very popular, and his "Cottage" is the resort of all whose business requires their attention along the river front. His Wines, Liquors and Cigars are selected with especial care as to their excellence and purity.

Mr. Arlow is the founder of his own property, and is entitled to great credit for the many business qualities he possesses.

## CAPITAL FLOUR MILLS.

### W. H. TENNEY & SONS.

Among the many celebrated Flour Mills of Georgetown, there is none whose specialties stand higher for purity, and command more ready market than these Mills.

W. H. TENNEY & SONS, owners and proprietors, established the Mills in 1870, and since then, have been constently employed in producing from one hundred to one hundred and twenty-five barrels per day. The special brands which have gained an extensive reputation for superior quality, and unsurpassed excellence, are Tenney's Hungarian Process, Tenney's Best Family and John Davidson's Family.

## SHIP AND CANAL STORES.

### A. H. BRADT.

One of the distinctive features of business in Georgetown, is that of supplying vessels and canal boats with all needful supplies. The most prominent establishment engaged in this class of business, is that of Mr. A. H. BRADT, who is located *on the Canal, near the Coal Elevators.* Here can be found every article needed by vessels and canal boats, including Groceries, Liquors, all kinds of Feed, Ship and Canal Stores. Mr. B. has an experience of over 27 years in this business, and is well qualified to realize the wants, and supply the demands of the trade. Mr. Bradt makes a specialty of the celebrated " Horsey Whiskey," from Burkettsville, Frederick County, Maryland. This is kept in stock and has an age of six years, also the " Golden Gate," this is purely a straight Rye Whiskey of superior quality and flavor.

## PIONEER MILLS.

### HERR & CISSEL.

Justly celebrated for the manufacture of Flour as Georgetown has become, no brands have attracted more attention and found their way to family use than those produced by the above Mills, this is in a great measure attributed to the present proprietors, Messrs. HERR & CISSEL. Mr. Geo. W. Cissel has spent a life-time in perfecting the different processes by which their brands are recognized, viz: Centennial 1st Premium, Great Swiss Process, Deener & Cissel Fancy, A. H. Herr's Best, and the Peerless Family Flours. Capacity of Mills, 300 barrels per day.

## BORDEN MINING COMPANY.

### S. H. SHERMAN, GENERAL SUPERINTENDENT.

This Company was organized in 1852, and located at Alexandria, Va., but was afterwards removed to Georgetown, in 1857. The Company was formed for the purpose of mining and supplying the eastern market with Cumberland Coal. Some idea of the extent of their operations may be inferred from the fact that they ship annually about one hundred and fifty thousand tons, giving employment to one hundred and fifty hands. Mr. S. H. SHERMAN the General Superintendent, has been connected with the Company ever since its formation, and is a gentleman of enlarged experience, and thoroughly posted in the affairs of the Company. He is assisted by W. H. MASTERS, son of the former agent.

Their office is located at the *Upper Coal Wharf, near the Coal Elevators.*

## AGRICULTURAL IMPLEMENTS AND FERTILIZERS.

### G. T. DUNLAP.

A farmer desirous of Implements of any kind, with which to plant, work or secure his crops, or Fertilizers that will both insure good crops, and permanently improve his lands, is compelled in a great measure to rely on the representations of the manufacturer. Such an establishment will be found at the *South-West corner Bridge and High Streets, Georgetown,* G. T. DUNLAP, Proprietor. Here he will find ever article useful upon a farm. Mr. Dunlap has an experience of twenty years in the business, and established the present house in 1870, and the extensive patronage enjoyed gives evidence of the superiority of its specialties. His stock embraces every thing in the line of Agricultural Implements, Machinery, Farmers' Hardware and Seeds, which comprises the largest and most carefully selected in the city. To give some idea of the varied assortment of articles on hand, mention may be made of the "Syracuse Chilled Plow," "Wheeler No. 6 Mower and Reaper Combined," "Osburn's Self-Binding Harvester," Single Reapers, Single Mowers, either front or rear cut, Whitinghouse Threshers and Cleaners, also his Improved Clover and Grain Threshers, Genuine Malta Shovel Plows, Portable Steam Engines, the Buckeye Grain and Phosphate Drill, Taylor's Horse Rakes, Corn Shellers, Hay Tedders, Wheat Fans, Hay and Fodder Cutters, Cucumber Wood Pumps, Harrows and Cultivators, Clover and Timothy Seeds, Garden Seeds, Plaster and all kinds of Guanos at Manufacturers' prices.

He is also the manufacturer of Dunlap's Maximum Fertilizer and Dunlap's Ammoniated Bone; these manures are carefully prepared, possess unusual strength, and wherever they have been thoroughly tested, are pronounced to be all that is claimed for them. First, that they are the best Fertilizers on the market, both as promoters of rapid growth of crops and permanent improvers of the soil. Second, that they are adapted to any crop, and farmers who have not given them a trial are advised to do so. Mr. Dunlap is a gentleman of enlarged experience and thoroughly acquainted with every detail of his extensive business, and farmers can depend on his representations.

## LUMBER TRADE.

### JOS. & J. E. LIBBEY.

One of the most interesting business features of Georgetown, is the trade in Lumber, for which her water facilities admirably adapt her. Among her most extensive and prosperous Lumber dealers, is the firm of Jos. & J. E. LIBBEY, whose father established the business now owned and controlled by them, nearly half a century ago. The magnitude of their operations may, in a degree, be estimated by the extent of their facilities for conducting them. They have three yards covering an area, in the aggregate, of over four acres, with a water front of two hundred and thirty feet, the whole of which space is occupied by them in their business. They give employment to a number of hands in the work of handling the lumber, and in performing the labor incident to the business of receiving and shipping. Their offices are located at 27 *Water Street*, and are handsomely and comfortably arranged for the rapid transaction of business, and the convenience of their customers. Their specialty is in Hard Wood Lumber, they being the only house in the District that keep on hand a constant supply of White Oak, Ash, Walnut, White and Yellow Pine, Shingles, Pickets, Laths, and all kinds of Building Lumber. Their trade extends to sections remote from Georgetown, though they chiefly supply the demands in the District and adjacent counties. The trade attractions of the establishment are unsurpassed, and the gentlemen of the firm are deserving of the success that has attended their energy and enterprise. In the office will be found a venerable attaché of the family and the business of the Messrs. Libbey, "Uncle Crusey," an old colored man, who for forty six-years has been unremittingly faithful to the trusts reposed in him by the father and sons in whose service he has worked, and of whose interests he has always been watchful. His fidelity has gained for him an affectionate place in the hearts of his "young masters," who reckon among their greatest pleasures, that of providing for his comfort.

## HARDWARE, IRON AND STEEL.

### H. P. GILBERT.

There is always some one in every city and town who by his ability and enterprise pushes to the front and becomes a public benefactor, by utilizing the facilities for trade and laying the foundations for increasing business and extension of labor. Prominent among this class of men appears the name of H. P. GILBERT, who located himself in Georgetown in 1863, at 93 *Water Street, near High,* where he has established a business that is second to none in the city. His business consists of Hardware, Iron and Steel of all sizes, either for sale or rent, including Blocks, Jacks, Dirt and Stone Barrows, Harness, Tug Boats, Scows, &c.

Some idea of the extensive nature of his business may be formed from the fact that he gives employment to from fifty to seventy-five men in the various branches of his extensive business.

Mr. Gilbert is engaged in many other industries that have for their object the improvement and prosperity of the community, foremost of which is the POTOMAC BLUE STONE QUARRIES, *on the Potomac River, located above Georgetown.* This Stone is of a bright blue color and is in every respect equal to granite, and can be cut into any shape. As a building stone, for durability and beauty it has no equal in this section of the country. The new Georgetown College is constructed from stone taken from these Quarries; it is also extensively used for foundations and paving purposes, and has given universal satisfaction.

Mr. Gilbert, by his liberal spirit and enterprise, has gained a wide-spread reputation for upright and honorable dealing. Several warehouses are brought into requisition for the requirements of his extensive business, including everything from a Nail to a Steam Engine.

He is also the builder and owner of several Boats that daily ply up and down the river, which are marvels of beauty, power and speed.

---

## CIGARS & TOBACCO.

### PETER J. MAY.

In some form or other, Tobacco has become of almost universal use; economy suggests the Pipe, but in this country, the greatest demand is exhibited for the Cigar. Mr. PETER J. MAY is a Practical Manufacturer of Cigars, and is located at 93 *High Street, Georgetown,* where he makes a specialty of the " Rose Bud; " this is a finely flavored Cigar, and gives great satisfaction to the lovers of the weed.

## GROCERIES AND LIQUORS.

### WILLIAM A. OFFUTT & BROTHER.

No one will deny that the most important business interests in any community are those which supply the public demand for food. The importance of purity and quality in every article of food, renders the business of supplying this demand one which should be entrusted only to reliable persons.

Representatives of this class of Merchants will be found in the firm of WILLIAM A. OFFUTT & BRO., *South-East corner Bridge and High Streets, Georgetown*, dealers in Fine Groceries, Liquors, and all kinds of Country Produce; among their various brands of Whiskeys, they make a specialty of the "Jockey Club" and "Baker" brands, both of which are fine and exquisitely flavored, and of the greatest purity. The business of this house was established in 1840, and after several changes, finally succeeded to the "Bros. Offutt." The Stock includes, beside all Staple Groceries, every thing coming under the head of "Fancy Groceries," which comprise Pickles, Sauces, Fancy Biscuits, Canned Fruits, etc.

The Messrs. Offutt are young men, who by energy and enterprise have established an extensive business throughout the County of Montgomery, and by their experience are better enabled to supply the wants of the Planters and Farmers, from the fact of their realizing their exact wants and desires. Such is the extent of their business, that they occupy the entire building of five stories, including the cellar.

---

## GRAIN, FEED AND HAY.

### D. B. JACKSON.

The facilities and improvements in Baling Hay and Grinding Feed for Stock, has improved so rapidly in the past few years, that this branch of trade has assumed important relations in the various branches of business. One of the largest and most extensive depots of this description is that of Mr. D. B. JACKSON, 110 *High Street, Georgetown*, Wholesale and Retail Dealer in all kinds of Grain, Feed and Baled Hay.

Mr. Jackson's enlarged experience in this branch of Business, is such as to guarantee purchasers that all articles sold are just as represented. This building is another of the old land-marks of Georgetown, having been built about seventy years ago, by Mr. Noble Hurdle, who is said to have shaken hands with every President save that of the present incumbent, Mr. Hayes.

## COMMISSION MERCHANTS.

### HARTLEY & BROTHER.

There is not a city in the country of its size that handles and manufactures as much Grain and Flour as Georgetown. The immense Flouring Mills, using hundreds of thousands of bushels annually—besides which the shipment, both by rail and water, open up a large and extensive field of operations for the Commission Merchant, Broker and Shipper. Prominent among this class of Merchants, from the extent of their business and commercial integrity, is the old and established firm of HARTLEY & BROTHERS, 95, 99, 101 *Water Street*, Dealers in Flour, Grain, and General Commission Merchants. This firm has been established since 1854, and occupy three warehouses with a combined capacity of storing thirty thousand bushels of Wheat.

## HYDRAULIC CEMENT & CALCINED PLASTER.

### J. G. & J. M. WATERS,

General Commisssion Merchants, and Agents for Round Top Hydraulic Cement and Red Beach Calcined Plaster, 28 *High Street, fronting immediately on the Chesapeake and Ohio Canal*, is one of the oldest Commission Houses in the City, having been established by Mr. GEO. WATERS some twenty years ago. All kinds of Grain is received on Consignment, and Cash Advances made and the interests of the Consignee carefully protected. They have several Warehouses, with a storage capacity of fifty thousand bushels. They are also extensive dealers in Red Beach Calcined Plaster and Cement.

## HATS, CAPS, &c.

### J. O. BARRON.

This business, especially in the large cities and towns, to be carried on successfully, requires persons of more than ordinary ability and judgment. As styles are constantly changing with every season, and as every one who purchases a hat desires to have one in the prevailing fashion, the dealer must exercise care and judgment in the selection of his stock, so as to be able to satisfy the demands of his customers. Mr. J. O. BARRON, 126 *Bridge Street*, from his long experience is eminently fitted for this branch of business, as his well selected assortment of Hats, Caps, &c., including Umbrellas and Canes, will attest.

11

## FAMILY GROCERIES.

## EUGENE T. LYDDANE.

A Family Grocery is an essential part of every community and of great convenience to families, farmers and planters who prefer to make small purchases and buy often, thus enabling them to have fresh and pure articles.  Such an establishment is that of Mr. EUGENE T. LYDDANE, 115 *High Street, Georgetown*.  His stock embraces every variety of Staple and Fancy Groceries, including Teas, Coffees, Sugars, Spices, Soaps, Starches, Canned Goods, Preserves, Jellies, Flour, Hams, Sides, Shoulders, &c.  Mr. Lyddane is a native of Montgomery, and has hosts of friends throughout the County, and as his store is located on the principal thoroughfare leading into the city from the County, it is no unusual sight to see the street in front of the store lined with wagons and carriages from the country.  The entire building, which is three stories in height, is occupied for carrying on the extensive business, including the Storage of Country Produce.  One hundred years ago this building was occupied as a public inn, and is one of the old land-marks of the city.  In the early colonial days it was a famous resort for the tobacco planters and farmers, where they used to congregate and discuss the topics of the day and relate the incidents of the last *fox hunt*.

---

## DRY GOODS, NOTIONS, &c.

## GIBBONS & BURROUGHS.

Of the entire commerce of the country, the trade in the above business in its extensive details is larger than that of any other, and no class of mercantile establishments contribute more to the life and prosperity of a City than those engaged in the sale of Dry Goods, Notions, &c.; nor do any class answer so important a purpose in advancing and promoting the business relations of a City.  In this department of trade and worthy of note is the firm of GIBBONS & BURROUGHS, 130 *Bridge Street*.  Their stock is the largest in the City, and is selected with especial care and adapted to the requirements of their customers, embracing both Foreign and Domestic, such as Ladies' and Gents' Furnishings, Black and Colored Dress Silks, Hamburg Laces, Ribbons, Housekeeping Linens, Notions, Sun Umbrellas, Black Crapes, White and Colored Dress Goods, Kid Gloves, &c.  The gentlemen comprising the firm have an experience of twenty-five years in handling this class of goods, which gives them great advantage in making their selections, being constantly on the look-out for novelties.  Combined with their facilities for conducting the business, they are enabled to offer inducements to purchasers that less favored houses are unable to do.  Entering the business when young men, they have grown up with Georgetown and have identified themselves with her material interests, and by enterprise and energy, have established a large and increasing business.

## NEW EXPRESS LINE.

### G. F. HYDE, AGENT.

This line was established in 1855, and has been an important factor in the industrial pursuits of the District of Columbia since that time.  The *Steamers of this line run between Georgetown, Washington, Alexandria and Philadelphia*, transporting between Philadelphia and intermediate points over twelve thousand tons annually, consisting principally of Flour from Georgetown, returning with General Merchandise.  Trips are made weekly each way.  The General Managers are W. P. CLYDE, 12 South Wharves, Philadelphia.  Mr. G. F. HYDE, the Agent in Georgetown, has had control of this end of the line for the past eight years, and by his energy and enterprise is due in a great measure the success of the Company.

## STEAM DYEING AND CLEANING.

### WILLIAM H. WHEATLEY.

The business or art of Dyeing and Cleaning, has grown to be a very important industry of this country, and affords means of subsistence to many worthy persons.  One of the oldest houses in this business, in the United States, is that of WILLIAM H. WHEATLEY, 49 *Jefferson Street, Georgetown*, which was founded by Mr. Wheatley's uncle in 1831, and has since that date enjoyed the entire confidence of the community, and a wide reputation for satisfactory execution of work.  The present proprietor succeeded to the business in 1855, and is constantly increasing the facilities, and enlarging the business relations of the house.  His trade is extensive throughout the District and adjacent States, nearly every mail or express receiving or delivering packages.  His building is large and commodious, where he employs a large number of the most skilled and practical dyers, and uses the most improved machinery, which is propelled by a forty horse-power engine.  In the Dyeing and Cleansing of Ladies' Dresses, Shawls, Sacques, Ties, Ribbons, Gents' Coats, Pants and Vests, the work is always done in a neat and durable manner; the colors being fast and will neither rub off nor fade.  Mr. Wheatley is a man that can be relied upon in every particular, and is worthy of a liberal patronage.

## RETAIL GROCERY.

### JOHN LYDDANE.

Dealer in Family Groceries, *South-West corner of High and First Streets, Georgetown*, adopted as his *watchword* "*Promptness*," over twelve years ago, and since that time has demonstrated the fact that purity of goods, and promptness in business transactions will assuredly be rewarded with success.

## MINERAL WATER MANUFACTORY.

### SAMUEL C. PALMER.

The popularity of Mineral Waters, combined with their health-giving properties, has created such an extensive demand, that establishments for their manufacture and bottling have been established in all the larger cities. One of the most extensive, South of Baltimore, is that of Mr. SAMUEL C. PALMER, 57 *Green Street, Georgetown*. He is also Agent for Massey's Philadelphia Ale and Schlitz's Milwaukee Lager. This business was established in 1862, and has been in successful operation ever since. Some idea of the extent of the business may be inferred from the fact that as many as two thousand dozen bottles have been delivered in a single day. Mr. Palmer also deals extensively in Bass' Ale, Guinness' Stout, Belfast Ginger Ale, Catawba Wine, Cider and Cider Vinegar.

## LAGER BEER BREWERY.

### MRS. SIMON DENTZE.

The consumption of Lager Beer in the United States has become so enormous in the past few years, that its production has became an important factor in the wealth of the country. In 1870, Mr. SIMON DENTZE established a Lager Beer Brewery, at 38, 40 and 42 *Green Street, Georgetown*, this was the first attempt at brewing Beer in the town; the experiment was successful.

Mr. Dentze, by his energy and the superior quality of his Beer, established a large and lucrative business, not only embracing the City of Georgetown and the surrounding country, but encroaching extensively on Washington City. At the death of Mr. Dentze, his wife took entire charge of the business, and has added many improvements. The Beer being manufactured strictly from pure Malt and Hops, is recommended by Physicians as a pure and efficacious tonic, for those who are suffering from debility.

# KAISER'S

## HOTEL AND RESTAURANT.

Farmers and those having business in Georgetown, will find comfortable quarters and good cheer, including Oysters in every style, Fish and Game in season at MR. KAISER'S HOTEL, 9: and 93 *High Street.* Mr. Kaiser came to Georgetown in 1853, and immediately identified himself with the interests of the people, and opened his present place in 1861. He is assisted by his son E. C. Kaiser, who is a "chip of the old block," and realizes the wants of the public, and by his pains-taking and courtesy has secured the mutual confidence of the public.

At his eating bar, Mr. Kaiser makes a specialty of Steamed Oysters, also Shucked Oysters supplied to families in any quantity.

Mr. Kaiser was placed in charge, in 1876, of the Agency of U. B. MUTUAL AID SOCIETY OF PENNSYLVANIA, the object of which is the relief of the families of its members after death. Eight dollars paid for membership and five dollars annually for four years, and two dollars annually during life, with a *pro rata* mortality assessment in case of death, will entitle each member to a certificate of one thousand dollars, to be paid at his death to his legal heirs, or assignees, whenever such event may occur. This Society is one that recommends itself to every one who desires to provide for his family in case of death.

# PROMINENT MERCANTILE FIRMS

## OF

# WASHINGTON, D. C.

---

## DRUGS AND CHEMICALS.

### STOTT & CROMWELL.

In all the large centres of population the Drug Business is of such a character and extent as to claim prominent position in the dominion of trade. The articles dealt in are of such a nature, and the relations existing between the Physician, Pharmacist and Jobber are such, that not only are the cardinal business virtues called for, but also a special knowledge of the qualities and properties of goods, such as is never required in general mercantile life.

When an enviable reputation and success has been acquired in this department of trade, it is evident that the essential qualifications above alluded to are possessed in a high degree, and such is the case with the house which is the subject of this sketch, Messrs. STOTT & CROMWELL, 480 *Pennsylvania Avenue.*

The business of this house was established by John F. Clark, and then succeeded by Mr. Stott in 1855, the senior member of the firm. The entire building is occupied by the various departments of their extensive business, consisting of the most complete assortment of Drugs, Chemicals and Patent Medicines, South of Baltimore. Three floors and the basement are heavily stocked with Chemicals, Drugs and Medicines, both those comprehended in the "*Materia Medica,*" and others of a proprietary nature. Many of the latter have been a long time before the public and have attained high and merited distinction. They are also extensive dealers in Mineral Spring Waters, including the celebrated Bethesda Waters, of which they are agents, which has gained such a world-wide reputation for the cure of Dyspepsia, Liver and Bilious Affections, and that much-dreaded "Bright's Disease" of the Kidneys, and Diabetes.

Their stock of Perfumery, Toilet Articles, Dye-Stuffs, Sponges and Chamois are large, and selected with special care for the requirements of their constantly increasing trade.

The business of the House in every respect is in a most flourishing condition. The members of the firm and salesmen are pains-taking and efficient, and it is but just to them to express the conviction that no more conscientious and capable representatives of a peculiarly responsible business can be found.

Farmers and Planters desirous of securing fresh Drugs and Medicines, will find it greatly to their advantage to visit the Store of the Messrs. Stott & Cromwell. Mr. Cromwell, the junior partner, is a native of Montgomery County, and has a lively interest in its future prosperity and growth. The gentlemen of the firm are experienced in the different branches of the business, and by their energy, enterprise and public spirit, have earned a reputation for honorable and fair dealing that has secured them their present position. May it continue to hold the reputation it has always enjoyed, as the Leading Drug House in the District of Columbia.

---

## "CONFECTIONERY."

### CARL MUELLER & SON.

The immense and constantly increasing demand for Confectionery of every description, both of French and American manufacture, has stimulated the energies of the people, who have in this respect put forth every effort that capital and enterprise, animated by the incentive that promotes the industrial millions of the Western Continent, to compete with Foreign Manufactories. The American Manufactories are far excelling the older establishments of the East, and her leading houses are now enjoying a world-wide reputation that gives evidence that they are not only able to compete with their Foreign competitors, but they are enabled, owing to central location and the production of the raw material, to manufacture an article that will stand the test of climate, and is capable of shipment to every part of the Globe. Notable representatives of Wholesale Confectioners in the District of Columbia, is Carl Mueller & Son, 314 *Pennsylvania Avenue, Washington, D. C.*, Manufacturers of French and American Confectionery, embracing every description of French Candies—including Caromels, Nut and Fruit Confections, Toy Candies, Sugar Kisses, Stick, Fragment and Rock Candies, including all the different flavors, with Gum and Fruit Drops in every conceivable shape—such as Pears, Peaches, Grapes, etc. They are also large and extensive dealers in Holiday Goods, such as Toys,

Fire-Works and Fruit Baskets, handsomely arranged and very artistic, suitable for presents and souvenirs.

Mr. Carl Mueller has a practical experience of thirty-five years as a Manufacturer of Confectionery, and through the assistance of his son, George J. Mueller, has been enabled to illustrate the fact that an establishment, founded on perfect business principles, combining the essential elements that contribute to the production of a pure article, will meet with that deserved success that always follows those who are deserving public patronage.

Their place of business is centrally located on the Avenue, occupying the entire building, including the extension built expressly for the purpose of introducing the modern improvements in machinery, and the appliances of skillful labor in the various branches of the business.

EXHIBITION AND SALES DEPARTMENT.—The first floor, on entering the store, presents a magnificent and varied appearance, being devoted to the display and sale of goods, embracing an assortment of every class of articles, both foreign and domestic. In the rear of which is located the office, which is conveniently arranged for the transaction of the immense business that is daily increasing.

The MANUFACTURING DEPARTMENT.—This building is of recent construction, and was built and arranged expressly for the manufacture of Pure Candies, and Confectionery; the basement of which is used for the storing of Molasses, Sugar and the raw materials used in the various branches of the manufactured articles. The first floor is used for receiving and packing, and is connected with the upper floors by an "Elevator," furnishing safe and rapid communication through the entire range of floors. Here also are found the great blazing furnaces, with "tanks" or "reservoirs" filled with boiling molasses and sugar, in front of which lay great broad cooling slabs of pure marble, on which the moulten compound is poured and allowed to cool.

The second floor is devoted to moulding the common and cheaper grades of Candy, or "Penny Goods" as they are known to the trade. Here also is located the machinery for grinding Cocoanuts and other articles required in making the many varieties that are found in their extensive catalogue. On this floor is located the great marble slabs upon which the Celebrated Chocolate Caramels, that have gained such a world-wide reputation, are spread and cut up.

The third floor is designated the " GIRLS' DEPARTMENT."—It is here that the fine French Rock and Fancy Candies are made and finished, Gum Drops and Kisses are wrapped and prepared for the market. The Starch and Drying Room is also located on this floor. None but the purest Sugar and Molasses are used by the Messrs. Mueller & Son, which accounts for the popularity of their goods and their rapidly increasing business. Such is the extent of his trade that he has four wagons constantly employed on the street delivering orders.

Mr. Mueller is as mindful of his Stock as he is for the comfort of his employés, for he has recently at great expense erected, in the rear of the manufactory, a large and handsome stable, for the accommodation of his horses. It is built in the most approved style, with a large ventilator extending from the lower floors where the stables are located, to the roof where it terminates in a handsome cupola. The floors are concreted, and the bins are self-supplying. The upper rooms are used for feed, harness, &c.

In conclusion, it is but just to say, that the remarkable success of this house must be attributed to the strict integrity of character, and faithful adherence to honest dealing that has always characterized their transactions.

The burden of the business falls on the shoulders of the son, Mr. Geo. W. Mueller, who is equal to the task, and in every way worthy the suc cess that has attended his efforts. A young man of great energy combined with strict business principles, he is sure to reach a proud position amongst the business men of the day.

---

## WHOLESALE GROCERS AND COMMISSION MERCHANTS.

### BARBOUR & HAMILTON.

In Groceries, Foreign and Domestic, Washington takes rank among the chief commercial Cities of the United States. Many of the most prominent business men who have given it high commercial standing, who have added millions to its substantial wealth, which in many cases they have nobly used for the City's general welfare and improvement, have been its Grocery Merchants. Prominent in this branch of business, not only as regards the volume of business transacted, the extensive stock on hand, and superior quality of their goods, but for sound integrity, and commercial standing as honorable and upright dealers, is the firm of BARBOUR & HAMILTON, 637, 639 and 641 *Louisiana Avenue, Washington, D. C.* This house was established in 1850, and since that time has been the leading Wholesale Grocery and Liquor Establishment in the District of Columbia. Recognizing the fact in the beginning that the Capital of the Country was destined to be one of the handsomest Cities in the World, and that her inhabitants would necessarily be comprised of the representative people, not only of the nation, but of the whole globe, they determined to establish business on a scale that would meet the requirements not only of the City, but one adapted to the wants and demands of the surrounding counties.  Their selections of Sugars, Teas and the Staple Articles of their Trade, embrace all the leading grades, and are sold at the same figures as those in the Eastern Cities, they being in constant communication with the principal foreign markets.  They are also extensively engaged as Rectifiers of Spirits and Wholesale Dealers in Liquors, of which mention may be made of Gaff Aurora Pure Rye Whiskeys, of 1873, '74 and '75 Vintage; John Gibson, Sons & Co., Whiskeys of all grades, at Distillers' prices; Martinsburg Pure Rye Whiskeys, Barbour & Hamilton's X, XX and XXX Rye Whiskeys; all of which can be purchased at prices as low as can be obtained from the Distillery.  They do an extensive business as agents in the Urbana Catawba Wines, Devoe's Brilliant Oil, (considered the *Safest Illuminator in the World*,) also for Harvest Queen Family, and Silver Spring Extra Flour.  A brand of Flour which calls for special notice is their " Our New West, " Patent Process Family Flour, which is unrivalled in the market.

Mr. Barbour attends to the financial department of the business, while Mr. Hamilton attends to the purchasing, and it will not be amiss to state that he is the best posted and closest buyer in the market.

---

## WHOLESALE GROCERIES AND LIQUORS.

### FRANK HUME,

Successor to Pool & Hume, 454 *Pennsylvania Avenue*, illustrates the fact that enterprise and energy, combined with strict integrity in business, is sure to meet with success.

The establishment of Mr. HUME is centrally located on the Avenue, and the several floors of the warehouse are occupied in the various departments of his extensive business, giving employment to a number of salesmen who are kept constantly employed in filling orders, both for City and Country.  Mr. Hume is thoroughly posted in every branch of the business, and persons can order from a distance, with the assurance that their wants will be supplied with first-class articles, and at prices that cannot fail to give entire satisfaction.  All goods are carefully packed and delivered without charge to the different wharves and depots.

Mr. Hume is Agent for Acme Family and Harper's Ferry Family and Extra Flour, and Mt. Summit and Brookfield Whiskeys.  These Whiskeys are especially adapted and suited for Family, Hotel and Bar use; also, the "Tom Moore" Pure Rye of 1868 Vintage.  Mr. Hume's assortment of Fancy Groceries, Canned Goods and Fruits is extensive, and selected with especial care to meet the wants of his customers.

## BOOTS AND SHOES.

### J. J. GEORGE.

The want of a perfect fitting Boot and Shoe, at the same time combining elegance of style and finish, is a want that most persons have experienced at some time in life. Mr. J. J. GEORGE, 2118 *Pennsylvania Avenue, North-West, Washington,* has a practical experience of eighteen years in the manufacture of Ladies' and Gentlemen's Footings. Mr. George uses none but the best of material in his work, and employs none but the most skilled and finished workmen in the various branches of the business. He pays special attention to the formation of the feet in taking his measure, and by a system which is of his own adoption, he is enabled to adapt the Boot or Shoe to the shape of the foot, thus ensuring an easy and well fitting article, that will never give pain or obstruct the easy grace and movement that lends such a charm to the graceful carriage of the promenader.

Mr. George has been for many years an exhibitor at the Montgomery County Fair, and by the superior excellence and durability of his work, established quite an extensive trade. He makes a specialty of Sportsmen and Farmers' Boots, who are compelled to be exposed to the snow and slush, and has prepared for their use a Leather Preservative and Waterproof Oil Composition, of which he is the Sole Manufacturer. The object of the Composition is to render the leather soft, pliable, waterproof and durable. He presents each purchaser with a box of this compound, which is found to accomplish all that is claimed for it. Such is the reputation of Mr. George for first-class work, that he is in daily receipt of orders from all parts of the country; officers in the Navy and Army ordering from their different Posts throughout the United States.

Another specialty which Mr. George pays great attention to, is Goat Skin Boots for Ladies, made strong and of exquisite finish, comfortable and durable, and in great demand during the winter.

---

## PAINTS, OILS AND VARNISHES.

### GEORGE RYNEAL, JR.

The use of Paints for the adornment of habitations and their surroundings, is at once beautifying, preserving and sanitary, and no one has contributed more to the improvement in this branch of business, than GEORGE RYNEAL, JR., Dealer in Paints, Oils, Window and Plate Glass, Lamp Goods, Artists' and Wax Flower Materials, etc., 639 *D Street,*

*North-West.* The entire three story building is filled with Goods, appertaining to his business. The commodious sales and display room is located on the first floor, and is under the immediate personal supervision of Mr. Ryneal, where will be found one of the largest and most complete assortments of Lamp Goods, Artists' and Wax Flower Materials in the City. The Paints, Oils and Varnishes are principally confined to the cellar, while the Window and Plate Glass, with the lighter articles of the trade, are distributed through the upper floors. He is also Agent for Johnston's Kalsomine and Fresco Paints and Masury Prepared Cottage Paints. Circulars, including Sample Colors, are sent on application.

Mr. Ryneal's business includes both a large City and Country trade, and by his indomitable spirit and enterprise, has acquired a reputation for strict integrity, fair dealing and business energy.

## HEATING AND COOKING STOVES.

### G. E. GARTRELL & CO.

The increase of manufactures and the rapid strides made within a few years past, in all branches of industry, has brought many improvements prominently before the public, none more so than those made in Heating and Cooking Stoves.

Prominent among those who have by their experience and practical knowledge introduced the improvements mentioned, are the Messrs. G. E. GARTRELL & Co., Dealers in Heating and Cooking Stoves, Latrobes and Furnaces, *No.* 1815 *Seventh Street, North-West.*

Mr. Gartrell has an experience of sixteen years in this business, and is well qualified to realize the wants of the public.

Their stock, which comprises one of the most complete in the City, embraces the Highland Queen, which is extra large, the Iron King, which is especially adapted for farmers who burn wood, the fire box being extra large and suitable to their convenience. In their extensive assortment, mention may be made of "Bibb's New Silver Palace," which is a fire-place stove, and combines all the features of old style, with the new improvements for heating rooms above.

They call the special attention of Farmers to the "*Harvest Home Range,*" which is very large and suitable for large families or boarding houses, &c.

Their stock of Household Furnishing Goods is very complete, including Tinware, Stove Fixtures, Wood and Willow Ware, and are sold at prices that are beyond competition.

The gentlemen comprising the firm are well known in Montgomery County, who by their pains-taking efforts have secured a large and lucrative trade.

## CLOTHING HOUSE.

### A. SAKS & CO.

Among the many changes that have taken place in the last century, no more radical revolutions has been accomplished than that in the cutting and making of gentlemen's garments. Ask your grandfathers or grandmothers what trouble there was to clothe the boys, and they will tell you that weeks of preparation were required to provide husband and children with the necessary Clothing for the season.

In that day the countryman and farmer who wore " store clothes " was considered a dandy, and the great improvement is due to such houses as that of A. Saks & Co. whose large establishments in Washington, Richmond and Lynchburg, afford such excellent means for those whose purse is either lean or fat, to be dressed in the most genteel and approved styles at a reasonable cost. The cutting, making and trimming departments necessary to produce the goods these large houses demand, are worthy of a visit, and some idea may be gained of the immensity of their trade.

When it is stated that notwithstanding all the labor-saving machinery employed, the firm have constantly at work on their goods no less than one hundred and fifty Tailors ; often this number is increased to two hundred and fifty. As Messrs. Saks & Co. are always courteous to visitors, those desirous of first-class articles will do well when next in Washington to call on them, and they will be seen to leave 310 *Seventh Street*, with pleasant recollections.

---

## CIGARS AND TOBACCO.

### GEORGE W. COCHRAN & CO.

The establishment of GEORGE W. COCHRAN & Co., Wholesale and Retail Dealers in fine Havana Cigars, Chewing and Smoking Tobacco, 1115 *Pennsylvania Avenue*, is the largest house South of Baltimore. Here the lover of the Weed can find every brand of Cigar, ranging from fifteen dollars to two hundred dollars per thousand.

Mr. G. W. Cochran, the senior member of the firm, established the business in 1847, and by strict attention to business and a quick perception to realize the wants of the public, has succeeded in building up the extensive patronage now enjoyed by the firm. Mr. J. W. Wetherall, who is associated with Mr. Cochran, is a practical and experienced Tobacconist, and devotes his exclusive time and attention to the details of the business. Mr. Cochran is a gentleman of enlarged business experience, and endowed with great executive ability, which has placed him at the head of several important enterprises, of which he is President.

## OYSTER TRADE.

### WILLIAM TURNER.

One of the important branches of trade in the District of Columbia, is that of Oysters and Fish. Some idea of the amount of business transacted in Oysters alone, may be inferred from the fact that over twenty thousand bushels of Oysters are brought to the wharves per week, from the 1st of September to the 1st of May, principally from the Potomac River and Chesapeake Bay.

One of the most prominent Dealers is Mr. WILLIAM TURNER, who does the largest business in the District, in supplying Hotels, Restaurants, Families, etc. Mr. Turner has an experience of twenty years in handling the Bivalves, and by his superior knowledge of the trade, combined with his energy and enterprise, has thus succeeded in establishing his extensive and lucrative business.

## GROCERIES AND LIQUORS.

### JOHN D. MANION,

Dealer in Groceries, Wines, Liquors and Cigars, *Corner Seventh and H Streets, two blocks from the Seventh Street Wharf,* has succeeded in establishing a large and increasing trade in Fine Family Groceries, Liquors, etc. His "Pimlico Club" and "Aurora" Whiskeys are pure, and are specially used for medical and family purposes. Persons visiting the City by boat will find a full and complete assortment of Staple Groceries, which Mr. Manion delivers free of charge and safely packed for transportation.

## FOREIGN AND DOMESTIC LIQUORS.

### CHR. XANDER.

It is of the utmost importance to the general trade throughout the country that the prominent and leading houses in the different mercantile pursuits should receive the acknowledgments of the public, provided they are deserving of it. Perhaps there is no class of merchants who are as liable to be mistrusted than those engaged in the Liquor Business—therefore a great deal of care and judgment is exercised by those who are desirous of selecting a reliable and responsible house to make their purchases. Such a gentleman and house will be found in Mr. CHR. XANDER, 911 *Seventh Street, North-West, Washington,* Distiller and Rectifier of all kinds of Domestic Liquors, and dealer in Foreign and Domestic Wines and Brandies. Mr. Xander has an experience of fifteen years, and by strict attention to business, has secured a reputation second to none.

His stock comprises the finest grades of Pure Old Rye and Bourbon Whiskeys. A specialty is made of the Old Gold Medal. These Liquors are distilled from the purest materials and are especially recommended for medical and family purposes.

He is also the Manufacturer of the Celebrated Tonic and Bitters, known as " Milliston," compounded from the juice of the Wild Cherry, with the extract of different herbs. As an appetizer, it is far superior in flavor and effect to those usually offered to the public. Planters from Montgomery County in search of fine Liquors should give Mr. Xander a call, where they will receive every attention and at the same time find it to their advantage, as he is sure to have exactly what they desire.

## WINE AND LUNCH ROOMS.

### MR. DAVID HAGERTY'S

Ladies' and Gentlemen's Lunch Rooms, *Corner 7th and E Streets*, is a popular resort for those who desire refreshments. Mr. Hagerty makes a specialty of Mixed Drinks, and after an experience of eighteen years, he certainly should be qualified to concoct a Punch or Julep.

## RESTAURANT.

### MR. W. H. WILKENING,

Proprietor of this popular resort, 337 *Pennsylvania Avenue*, is prepared at all times to furnish the choice selections of the season, including the finest of Wines and Liquors.

## "HOLE IN THE WALL."

### FRANK HAGERTY.

This Restaurant is presided over by the popular FRANK HAGERTY, and is located at 454 *Louisiana Avenue, opposite the City Hall.* The usual discount of fifteen per cent. allowed on coin and currency.

## COLLECTION OFFICE.

### WILLIAM H. BENNETT,

Constable and Collector, 476 *Louisiana Avenue.* Business intrusted to Mr. Bennett will meet with prompt attention and quick returns.

## CLARK HOUSE.

### MR. LAWRENCE CLARK,

For twenty-five years a resident of the District, has established himself in the above house, *Corner 7th and L Sts., South-West, opposite the River Front.*

John L. Clark, formerly of 6th and C Streets, North-West, chip of the old block, presides in the office, where his friends will be sure of a hearty welcome.

---

## AMERICAN HOUSE.

### DUFFY & LEANNARDA.

The American House, *Corner of Pennsylvania Avenue and Seventh Street,* is the oldest established house in Washington, and having been recently renovated and refitted, this house is prepared to offer great inducements to the public.

To parties desiring to enjoy a few days in the city, this house especially commends itself, combining home comforts with a Hotel table. Being centrally located, within five minutes walk of all Railroad and Steamboat lines, convenient to the Government Departments, and Street Cars passing the door in all directions.

To those of their old patrons in the County who have been familiar with the House for years past it is unnecessary to speak further, and to their friends, the Messrs. DUFFY & LEANNARDA promise careful attention and a determination to please.

---

# FREDERICK, MARYLAND.

## "DILL HOUSE"

### PICKING & DEAN.

This popular House has recently been refurnished and renovated throughout, while its central location, being in close proximity to the Court House and Banks, makes it a desirable resort for those whose business requires them in this direction. The Proprietors, Messrs. PICKING & DEAN. are gentlemen who know the requirements of guests, and are always on the alert to supply their wants. Mr. Dean is a host within himself, and from long experience is well qualified to realize the wants of the public. He is the right man in the right place.

# FULLNAME INDEX

BELT (cont.)
W M 139
BENNETT, John A 136 R H
131 William 103 William H
167
BENSON, 99 103 J E 131 J N
135 John T 131 Johnson
135 Thomas E 135 Wm H
131
BENTLEY, 141 R T 38
BENTLY, Caleb 91 93 Richard
T 96
BENTON, James N 126
Thomas 108
BERGER, 137
BERRY, J D 137 John 84 129
John Summerfield 84 Thos
L 84
BIAYS, J P 140
BIGGS, Isaac 91
BITZER, 138
BLACK, William 45
BLACKWITH, W T 133
BLAIR, F P 29 Francis P 92
Montgomery 29 67 111 142
BLAKE, George 133
BLUNT, W W 131
BOARMAN, Robert 129
BOHER, Julius 144
BOHRER, J T 120 John G 120
BOLINGER, W 120
BOND, J L 142 James H 129
James L 129 William 37
BONE, Allen 123
BONIFANT, George 125 James
36
BORDLEY, Thomas 39-40
BOSWELL, Frank 137 James
139 Nicholas 143 R K 122
BOTELER, A J 134
BOUIC, 139 D H 140 Judge 34
44 Rufus A 135 W V 140 W
Veirs 111
BOWIE, Allen 51 144 Col W
137 Henry 129 R I 140
Richard I 41 Richard J 67
111 Rufus A 127

BOWLEN, G W 119
BOWMAN, Asbury 124 Frederick 119
George W 134 Rezin H 126 U 139
Uriah G 131 William 144
BOYD, Elizabeth 125 James A 81 121
John 41 R T 41 95 Reuben T 85-
87 T H S 60 85 107 113 125
BOZZELL, J Q 143
BRADDOCK, Gen 50
BRADFORD, John 33 38-39 46
BRADHSAW, John 83
BRADLEY, George 44 George G 137
Henry 137 Henry Jr 137 Joseph
120 Joseph H 106 W P 125
BRADT, A H 148
BRALL, Rufus 127 Wm 127
BREADY, C W 139 John 141 S K 139
BREATON, W 144
BRENGLE, J H 132
BREWER, 103 139 D N 121 George
138 John 68 John B 140 Nicholas
68 W G 120 William 138
BRIAN, John M 128
BRIGGS, Gideon 130 James M N 130
John 130 Robert 130 Samuel 130
Thomas 130
BRIGHTWELL, Richard 31
BRISCOE, Robert 58
BROOKE, Alban 141 Albin 136 C F
137 Charles 39 Charles F 141
Edmond 44 Edmund 32 George E
141 James 25 39-40 Mary 90
Richard 37 51 58 Robert 22 40
Roger 33 90 92 136 Thomas 30 W
S 140 William S 33
BROON, Duthorn 126
BROPLEY, Samuel 146
BROWN, 103 Abel 46 B Peyton 116-
117 D W 133 Edward 134
Franklin 143 J H 143 Joshua 143
M J 133 Nancy 38 Ridgely 60
Robert 40 143 Thomas 144 Uriah
143 William 39 William W 143
BROWNING, Charles T 132
BUCHANAN, George 47
BUDD, Samuel 141 Thomas 141
BUOY, Michael 82

3610900

Made in the USA